What readers are saying about Dr. Gary Rodriguez's *Purpose-Centered Public Speaking....*

"In Purpose-Centered Public Speaking, *Gary Rodriguez takes the fear out public speaking. Relating years of public speaking experiences, Gary provides a great game plan for you to become a fearless public speaker. His insights and wisdom will certainly make you a better public speaker. He will also make you a stronger communicator in all areas of your life."*
– Brent Jones, Former San Francisco 49er Tight End and Winner of Three Super Bowl Rings

*"*Purpose-Centered Public Speaking *offers aspiring as well as active speakers valuable tips and techniques for improving their communication skills. In addition to the helpful instruction, you will also find this book highly entertaining. If you are a public speaker this is a book you should read."*
– Stephen G. Newberry, President & CEO Lam Research Corporation, Fremont

"Don't just read this book. Digest and practice the principles recorded here, and soon you will find an increasing ease in communicating and a more favorable response from your listeners."
– Wayne Cordeiro, Founding Pastor of New Hope Christian Fellowship, Honolulu

"This book is so much more than a 'how to' on public speaking! Rodriguez inspires the reader through compelling stories both deeply personal and at times universal. Anyone who wants to feel at ease in front of audiences will gain strength, encouragement and useful resources and tools on how to step into the spotlight and create rapport and connection with one's listeners."
– Pamela Mclean, CEO, Hudson Institute of Santa Barbara

"I found Dr. Rodriguez's book, Purpose-Centered Public Speaking, *a superb 'how to' guide to public speaking. The book held my interest by using interesting real life examples and very practical tips that any speaker can learn from. It takes the mystery out of how to prepare and deliver a compelling speech with a purpose. Whether you are preparing for a talk at a family gathering or regularly find yourself in front of an audience at work, this book will help you deliver a focused message that hits home."*

– Bill Munger, Chief of Staff and Vice President of HR EnergyConnect, San Jose

*"*Purpose-Centered Public Speaking *is a wonderful book for speakers and an enjoyable read. Written with warmth and humor, it is enlightening, encouraging, and refreshing, offering great concepts and principles that can work in all aspects of our lives."*

–Maggie Williams, Chief Administration and Finance Officer, Catholic Charities, SSC

"Gary's systematic methods for public speaking are practical, easy to understand, and presented with relevant illustrations that will help anyone create a better presentation, whether you're a business leader or school teacher."

– Steven J. McGriff, Ph.D., Instructional Technologist, Krause Center for Innovation, Foothill College, Los Altos Hills, CA

"This approach to public speaking is refreshing and insight-ful—from the 4 vital questions to creating a purposeful talk with a strong introduction, pointed illustrations and action-oriented conclusion. This book will enable critical skills for anyone want-ing to create a purposeful, practical and productive speech."

– Martin Woodrow, President, Martin Consulting Solutions, Inc., San Jose

"This book provides a solid foundation on the fundamentals of public speaking for those who only speak in public on occasion and a helpful refresher for those of us that speak to groups regularly. I highly recommend it."
– Jeffrey J. Rodriguez, President, Brown & Riding Insurance Services, Inc., Los Angeles

*"*Purpose-Centered Public Speaking *is a fun and engaging read, and Dr. Rodriguez does a nice job of humanizing the subject. He gets to the heart of the matter by offering actionable ways to feel more comfortable with public speaking. I now utilize his approach when I speak in front of groups, and I am finally starting to enjoy public speaking again."*
– Lynn Fischer, VP Sales and Marketing, Title 21 Software, Inc., Las Vegas

"I can honestly say that I had an epiphany as I read your book that will benefit both my organization and me for the years to come. Your 'Model Message' on Vision was not only convincing but it was also very timely."
– Frank Velasquez, President and Managing Partner, Cornerstone Technologies, LLC., San Jose

"What impresses me most about Purpose-Centered Public Speaking *is that the challenge of effective public speaking is made so simple, understandable, and doable. Gary Rodriguez gives practitioners' useful and pragmatic tools and techniques that they can immediately use for all contexts of speaking and presentations. This book gives me the tools and the confidence to greatly improve my own public speaking skills and effectiveness."*
– Thomas G. Peterson, Former Product Division General Manager, Applied Materials, Inc., Santa Clara

Purpose-Centered Public Speaking

Purpose-Centered Public Speaking

How to Develop and Deliver
Purposeful Talks, Speeches, and
Presentations with Less Fear
and More Confidence

Dr. Gary Rodriguez

Published by LeaderMetrix, Incorporated
www.LeaderMetrix.com

Printed in the United States of America

ISBN-978-1-4507-2708-2
First Printing: August 2010

Library of Congress Control Number: 2010911005
Library of Congress Subject Headings:
Purpose-Centered Public Speaking
Communication
Business

Cover design by Hope Nixon
Editing by Barbara Brabec

Dedication

This book is dedicated to my fair Colette. Throughout my life, I have known many friends. Most of them have come and gone like changing seasons. Some special friends have endured. They have loved me, and I have loved them, for more years than I can count. Even so, you, my dear one, are like no other. You are as faithful as you are good. Thanks for your tireless love, unwavering friendship, and pure-hearted devotion over these many years. I will also not soon forget the countless times you proofread this manuscript in an effort to make it right. This book is not only mine. It is truly ours!

Brandi and Paul—through the bumps and bruises of life we have remained constant together. We have loved, laughed and cried during the best and worst of times. If I could do it all over again, surely it would be with the two of you again by my side.

Grandchildren are truly a blessing. There are five who bring great joy to me: Ashley, Isabella, Madeline, Jake, and Addison. May your minds grow strong and your hearts grow stronger. Thinking of each of you brings a smile to my face.

Table of Contents

Acknowledgments

I would be remiss in not mentioning some of the people who have contributed to my growth as both a person and a presenter over the years. They include Dr. Haddon Robinson, Wayne Cordeiro, Earl D. Radmacher, and Dr. Peter Wilkes, who personally and patiently mentored me in matters of life as well as the art of public speaking.

Special thanks goes to Martin Woodrow for his support during this arduous process and to my editor, Barbara Brabec, for her special contributions.

If you find this book useful, please give the above individuals a good share of the credit. On the other hand, should you find flaws or miscues on any of the following pages, the fault is solely mine. May the time you invest in this book pay great dividends in your future endeavors as a public presenter.

Preface

In some ways, this book is a glimpse into my life's story. It celebrates my continuing journey and ongoing development as a public speaker, but it is more a story about my process than it is about my arrival.

There are literally thousands of books on public speaking, so why is this one worthy of your time? Like most people, public speaking did not come easy for me. Once upon a time, the very thought of talking in public would make me apprehensive and a bit sweaty. Nevertheless, public speaking is kind of like death and taxes; there is no way around it.

Books are plentiful that focus on preparing presentations and delivering them with skill and style. This book, which is directed to active and aspiring speakers, teaches one how to build a purpose-centered presentation from start to finish. My goal here is to offer the reader a proven systematic approach designed to help new and experienced speakers develop and deliver purposeful talks that produce a desired outcome. This purpose-centered approach gives speakers an upfront goal that helps them align all components of the talk so that they achieve a predetermined result.

In a busy world, sometimes we need a thumbnail sketch of a subject, one that shows us a view of the big picture albeit in a small and condensed way. Thus this book is designed to be more of an overview than a treatise on public speaking. I trust you will use the helpful resources included herein to continue your study of this fascinating topic.

Foreword

E ver watch a skilled concert pianist? His fingers glide over the ivories leaving behind a wake of enchanting melody. The movements seem effortless, and every motion produces a bouquet of harmony.

But this does not come automatically.

This kind of freedom is actually birthed from the disciplined sequence of endless scales. Again and again, specific scales are repeated as a doting instructor closely scrutinizes each movement. The deliberate fingerings continue *ad infinitum*, but as the student's discipline increases, so does his fluidity. The *do-re-mi-fa-so-la* hours of practice give way to moving arpeggios and swaying legatos. And soon, purposeful practice rewards a lucky audience to an enchanting evening of music.

The same is true with communicating.

Watch a professional. The speaker moves an audience to laughter or tears. He compels a group to action or takes them down a nostalgic journey in history. He guides them on an uncharted adventure, paints a story, or opens their ears to a symphony.

And he makes it look so simple.

But, like the concert pianist, the ease in presentation does not come automatically. It begins with discipline and adhering to the basic principles of communication.

What you hold in your hands is a book that will help you recognize those basic principles. It will guide your ability to communicate in the right way. It will show you the mechanics of speaking, and, if followed, will increase your chances for success in your organization, church, or community group.

Don't just read it. Digest and practice the principles recorded here, and soon you will find an increasing ease in communicating and a more favorable response from your listeners.

Gary Rodriguez is one of those who makes it look so easy. Learn the principles and join the growing number of people who have unlocked the secrets to successful communicating.

The keys are here . . . your symphony awaits.

Wayne Cordeiro
Founding Pastor of New Hope Christian Fellowship,
Honolulu, HI

Introduction

"WHILE WE ARE FREE TO CHOOSE OUR
ACTIONS, WE ARE NOT FREE TO CHOOSE
THE CONSEQUENCES OF OUR ACTIONS."
– Stephen Covey

Sooner or later, you will be asked or forced to speak in a public setting. Although this thought exhilarates some, it terrifies most. Fear of public speaking silences many voices. Unfortunately, this type of silence can limit your career, influence, and potential for success.

Most likely, you picked up this book because you either want or need to learn to speak in public. No matter the reason, here you will find practical insights and tools designed to improve your ability to speak in front of others.

Speaking in public is not rocket science. Yet, becoming a proficient speaker does require a serious commitment to learn, as well as a fair amount of practice. I have been involved in public speaking for over thirty-five years, yet, my growth as a speaker is continuously developing. Every time we speak in public there are new opportunities to develop and refine our communication skills.

Generally, speakers learn their craft in two ways: mentoring and consequences. Mentoring happens when we study and learn from talented communicators who tutor us in skills and techniques that develop us as presenters. In addition, listening to their wise counsel helps us avoid foolish and unnecessary mistakes. Conversely, consequenc-

19

es are sure to follow when we fail to learn from those who have mastered the art of communication before us. Mentors teach and inspire us, but consequences are hard taskmasters. They exact their pound of flesh with every painful lesson. The good news is that the more we embrace mentoring, the less the belt of consequences schools us.

Much of what you read in this book is wisdom gleaned over the years from valued and trusted mentors. Some of what is written, however, I learned from consequences suffered.

When it comes to public speaking, I consider myself a veteran, rather than an expert because I still have so very much to learn. Yet the tools and techniques I've gathered along the way do equip me to provide valuable help to both active and aspiring speakers. My motive for writing this book is simple. I want to "pay it forward," and this endeavor is my way of saying thanks to the mentors who have tutored me along the way. These talented men and women have patiently instructed me in the art of communication, have graciously taught me practical wisdom, and kindly given me insights into their own unique presentation styles.

Over the years, I have listened to speakers both good and poor. The good ones have taught me what I aspire to do, while the poor ones have illustrated things I want to avoid.

Public speaking demands a combination of courage and skill. You have already demonstrated bravery by picking up this book. If reading what follows empowers you and improves your ability to speak in public, then this writing will have served its intended purpose.

20

CHAPTER ONE

Courage Under Fire

"COURAGE DOESN'T ALWAYS ROAR.
SOMETIMES COURAGE IS THE QUIET VOICE
AT THE END OF THE DAY SAYING, 'I WILL
TRY AGAIN TOMORROW.'"
– Mary Anne Radmacher

He knew she would call on him. First the old nun glanced left, then right. He was doing his best to hide. Even so, he knew she would find him. For a second he thought, maybe I'm wrong. Perhaps she will pick someone else. He slumped even lower in his chair, shielded by a row of classmates. Unfortunately, he made the fatal mistake of peeking out at the wrong time. In an instant, their eyes met. She called him by name and asked him to stand in front of the class. There was no way out. Reluctantly, he stood to his feet and slowly walked to the head of the class. He didn't need to look to know that all eyes were upon him. His heart was now beating like a rabbit's.

Finally, the teacher said the dreaded words, "Class, open your readers to Lesson 3." Then she told the terrified second grader to read aloud to the class. Hesitantly, he began to read, stumbling over nearly every word. In seconds, silent snickers turned to open laughter. Even the old nun could not contain herself. After what seemed like an eternity, he quit reading and somehow found his way back to his seat. Humiliated, he slid down into his chair wishing he could disappear. Second graders can make vows, and on that day he vowed never to read aloud or speak in a public setting again. And for many years he kept that vow. However, as an adult, things changed. His role in the military forced him to do what he vowed never to do. He has been speaking in public ever since, hundreds of times to thousands of people. This story is true. It is my story. I was that little second grader. Take it from me, if I can learn to speak in public, so can you.

Wrestling with Fear

Jerry Seinfeld got a big laugh when he joked about a survey that found that the fear of public speaking ranks higher in most people's minds than the fear of death. "In other words," he deadpanned, "at a funeral, the average person would rather be in the casket than giving the eulogy."
– Jerry Seinfeld[1]

Fear is our natural response to danger. Like that little second grader, many believe public speaking is terrifying and risky, and statistics verify this point. On May 14, 2010, *USA Today Snapshots* listed activities adults say they dread and public speaking was at the top of the list.[2]

It is well known that fear of public speaking ranks up there with fear of death, snakes, and spiders. Why is it that speaking in front of a group of people solicits such fright and dread? Let us begin by attempting to answer this question.

---

1 www.time.com/time/magazine/article/0,9171,994670-1,00.html
2 TNS for LG Spring Cleaning Survey of 1,000 adults, March 2010.

Glossophobia, or speech anxiety, is the fear of speaking in public. Wikipedia lists symptoms related to this phobia as "intense anxiety prior to, or simply at the thought of, having to verbally communicate with any group; physical distress, nausea, or feelings of panic."

If you have ever experienced these symptoms, you are not alone. Most speakers wrestle with anxiety to a greater or lesser degree. Some speakers do so before, others during, and still others after speaking engagements.

Although speech anxiety is common, it should be differentiated from other phobias such as "social phobias" or "social anxiety disorders." These phobias have to do with fear of crowds, and they can certainly add fuel to the fire when it comes to a speaker's anxiety. People with social anxieties experience emotional and bodily discomfort just by entering a crowded setting. Often this is true whether or not they are scheduled to speak. Social phobias complicate a public speaker's task, but they can be overcome. (Severe social anxieties, however, are best treated with the help of a trained professional.)

Generally, speaking in public is not hazardous to your health, and it won't kill you, although there have been exceptions. For instance, Jesus Christ, Dr. Martin Luther King, and a host of other historical figures whose messages inspired, and often

Check out the "Fear of Public Speaking Phobia Self-Help Test" in the Appendix or visit www. speech-topics-help.com and take the test online.[1]

---

1 Special thanks to Jim Peterson for giving me permission to use the "Fear of Public Speaking Phobia Self-Help Test." Visit www.speech-topics-help.com for a variety of support and help for public speakers.

enraged, the masses. Their words evoked such faith and allegiance that many loyal followers were willing to die in order to perpetuate their teachings. Those who opposed them committed violent acts, even murder, in the vain hope of silencing them. In the end, their deaths only served to magnify their teachings. It is fair to say that most of us need not worry about suffering bodily harm as a result of speaking in public, so that is one bit of fear we can put behind us.

> *"Our deepest fear is not that we are inadequate. Our deepest fear is that we are powerful beyond measure. It is our light, not our darkness that frightens us most. We ask ourselves, 'Who am I to be brilliant, gorgeous, talented, and famous?' Actually, who are you not to be? You are a child of God. Your playing small does not serve the world. There is nothing enlightened about shrinking so that people won't feel insecure around you. We were born to make manifest the glory of God that is within us. It's not just in some of us; it's in all of us. And when we let our own light shine, we unconsciously give other people permission to do the same. As we are liberated from our own fear, our presence automatically liberates others."*
> *– 1994 inaugural speech by Nelson Mandela*

A Few Words about Courage

Some people think the opposite of fear is the absence of it. It is not. The opposite of fear is *courage*. Permit me to share a personal story that might be helpful at this point.

Many years ago, I fought in the Viet Nam war, serving in the United States Army as the Staff Sergeant of a twenty-eight-man helicopter assault platoon. I was twenty-years old at the time, and my platoon was a rapid deployment force assigned to protect the 4th Division in the Central Highlands of Viet Nam. We had four helicopters that transported us into battle and two Cobra gun ships that acted as escorts. During my tour of duty, I was awarded the Silver Star, the nation's third highest award for valor under fire.

I remember that day like it was yesterday. We were on patrol in a dense jungle when suddenly all hell broke loose. In a moment, the air was filled with the smell of burned gunpowder from firing weapons. This pungent smell was mixed with the odor of sweaty men and a myriad of jungle scents. It was my responsibility to lead, but at that moment all I wanted to do was hide. During the firefight, I carried a wounded comrade to a medical evacuation helicopter. On returning to base camp, I learned that men in the field had recommended me for the Silver Star.

The day the award was given, I stood in a short line with four or five other soldiers who were also receiving commendations. When the senior officer came to me, I felt like an imposter because the level of fear I experienced on the battlefield that day had made me feel more like a coward than a hero. Yes, I did what it said on my certificate, but the officer had no idea how frightened I was at the time. As

> *Courage is not the absence of fear; on the contrary, courage is doing the right and honorable thing in the midst of extreme fear.*

he pinned the Silver Star to my chest and told me that I was a war hero, I recall blurting out, "I was so afraid; I'm no hero."

I will never forget his next words. "Yes, son, you are a hero, because when overwhelmed by fear, your courage prevailed and you performed a heroic act." To this day, I am proud and grateful for the Silver Star because it constantly reminds me of the true definition of courage.

Public speakers need courage because most will face some degree of fear and/or anxiety before, during, or after they speak. For some, that fear may be related to a concern about failing and the subsequent rejection that might follow.

Stop for a minute and ask yourself these questions: *What is the worst thing that can happen to you?* What if you stand in front of a group of people and mess up? What if you get lost during your talk or forget what you wanted to say? What if you look out into the audience and everyone looks bored?

Questions like these surface in all of us, but notice the common denominator: *It is simply the fear of humiliation.* Our pride says, "If you don't try, you can't fail," and this is what keeps so many voices silent. Perhaps your motto has been, "Better to remain quiet and let people think I'm a fool, than to open my mouth and prove them right."

Can speakers humiliate themselves in front of a crowd? Yes, it does happen, but not as often as you might think. Most people in an audience realize the difficulties related to speaking in public, and this generally makes them more tolerant and forgiving than you might imagine. Remember, with few exceptions, more people will be rooting for you rather than against you.

Improving Content and Presentation Skills

Those new to public speaking should focus on improving both the quality of their content and the skill sets associated with presenting it. One way to improve the quality of your content is to increase the time you spend researching your topic. The more knowledgeable you are on a given subject, the more credible you will be to the audience. Credibility intensifies your listeners' interest and desire to hear what you have to say. Increased knowledge of your subject will also heighten your level of confidence as a presenter.

The other half of the equation is strengthening your presentation skills, and there are a couple of ways it can be done. Begin by observing other presenters. Watching seasoned veterans speak will help you to see how the "pros" do it. Nowadays, you can watch videos online of some of the best speakers in the world. When you see them in person or on video, scrutinize them. Watch their gestures, where they focus their eyes, and how they use the podium (platform or stage). Listen for changes in inflections, tempo, and generally observe how they use their

> *Make the commitment never to do inadequate or shoddy research. Presenters guilty of this transgression do both listeners and themselves a great disservice. Know what you are talking about!*

voice. Observe how they incorporate humor, raise the intensity level, and ask and answer questions. Watching them will give you insight into why they are so effective. They will also provide you with useful tips for improving yourself.

> *No speaker is perfect. Some are great at gathering content but are short on presentation skills. Other speakers are charismatic presenters, yet they struggle when it comes to developing quality content. Again, very few speakers have it all together. As Ralph Waldo Emerson reminds us, "All great speakers were bad speakers first."*

Video Self-Critiques

Another way to become a better presenter is by watching yourself. The easiest way to do this is by using a video camera and recording your presentations. I highly recommend that you make video critiques an ongoing practice. They will prove to be extremely helpful because you will quickly discover the good, the bad, and the ugly about the way you present. Remember, when you critique yourself, it is imperative that you notice your strengths and not just your weaknesses. Spend at least as much time developing the things you do well as you do shoring up the things you need to improve.

Be Yourself

My home is located a stone's throw from the Silicon Valley in San Jose, California. Several years ago I met an engineer who was struggling with public speaking at work. Although he was brilliant, he was far from what anyone would consider charismatic. Try as he did, he could not figure out how to become like other presenters he admired. Everyone praised the quality of his content but agonized over his boring presentation style. This dilemma almost cost him his job and ended his public speaking career.

Our initial focus was centered on his content rather than his presentation skills. First, we switched the way he formatted his content from outline form to "movements" (more on this later). Second, he learned the strategy of "beginning at the end" (more on this topic in Chapter 4). This preliminary work helped his presentations become more purpose-centered while also improving their structure. This in turn elevated his level of confidence and relieved some of the fears that continually dogged him.

By then, we were free to look at other issues. Intuitively, I sensed a veiled problem. "Tell me the name of a presenter that you admire," I suggested, and he named a woman at work he considered a magnetic and captivating speaker.

"Do you think you can learn to be like her?"

After thinking a minute, he said, "Honestly, no."

Then I asked him to give me the name of someone else he might aspire to be like, and he mentioned John Maxwell, a popular speaker in corporate circles. When I asked if he thought he could become a presenter like John Maxwell, given time, he lowered his head and said after a short pause, "I guess not."

Knowing I was gradually bringing him to an important point of understanding, I asked, "If you can't be like the woman at work, and you can't be like John Maxwell, who can you be?" He looked visibly frustrated and a bit discouraged as he said, "I can't be like anyone." I repeated his last words, "like anyone?" Then he looked up and said, "All I can be is me."

On hearing those words I grinned and said we were now ready to get started. The lesson here is that all we can be is who we are. That is where we have to start. Aspire to be the best "you," and leave the rest to someone else.

Years ago, as a younger speaker, this same lesson was driven home for me. It happened shortly after meeting one of the best speakers I had ever heard. After deciding I was going to be just like him, I made several adjustments to my style and delivery in hope of being more like this "master." Soon people were noticing the difference, but not in the way I had hoped. Instead of compliments, I started getting comments like, "What happened to you? You don't seem like yourself." At this point, you might think I would have abandoned my plan to mimic this guy, but sadly I did not. Instead, I decided I needed to try even harder to be like him. It was a stupid decision. Things went from bad to worse. Eventually, I discovered the same lesson my engineer friend had to figure out. I could only be me.

Remember earlier when I talked about learning some things by painful consequences? Well, this is a great example. *Do not waste your time trying to be someone else. Learn who you are as a speaker and grow from there.* Who knows, someday someone might try to imitate you.

> "Be who you are and say what you feel because those who mind don't matter and those who matter don't mind."
> – Dr. Seuss

30

The Engineer's Success Story

There are thousands of effective and successful speakers all around us. Not all of them have "famous" names. Many are average men and women who have learned to communicate in public effectively. My engineer friend is one of them. He eventually discovered that he had a dry sense of humor, a gift for mimicking voices, and a genuine likeability. Over time his presentation style changed for the better. It all began when he decided to be "himself."

The payoff began on a day like any other. He was slotted to speak for twenty minutes. Walking to the podium, as usual, he felt anxiety and some fear. The room was filled with a gathering of less than eager attendees. Normally, his dry and boring talks would begin and within minutes the yawning would start. On this morning, he opened his talk using a very different approach than normal. He started with a new degree of transparency and bit of humor. Below is a paraphrase of what he said:

> *Good morning, thanks for being here with me. I have so much I want to say today that's vital to this company's success, as well as your own. I will talk more about that in just a minute. However, first, I'd like to make a personal confession. It has taken me a while, but I have discovered I'm a rather boring public speaker. At first, it was hard for me to admit this to myself, but I have finally done so. The other evening I tried to watch a video of myself speaking. I nodded off after about five minutes and had my best night's sleep in months. [Laughter] If I asked for a show of hands, I bet most of you would*

agree with me that I am a rather boring presenter. Now here is the good news. I have hired a speaking coach to help me improve. I can't make any promises, but I can guarantee you this: If any of you go to sleep during the next twenty minutes, the rest of us will find out if this new Taser Stun Gun I bought really works. [Laughter]

According to my engineer friend, the Taser line brought the house down. He had never before tried to say anything remotely funny in a presentation, at least, not intentionally, but when he did, his colleagues howled with laughter. For the next twenty minutes, his talk was seasoned with quality content and a more authentic and humorous style. He wasn't accustomed to seeing everyone's eyes open at the same time. They were uncharacteristically interested in hearing what he had to say, and he joked that his Taser Stun Gun stayed in the holster the remainder of the day (of course, he never really had one).

In the interest of full disclosure, my engineer friend will never make his living as a public speaker, but he did learn to become a respectable presenter, and this qualifies as a win. He has learned courage under fire. Yes, there is still a degree of fear and anxiety whenever he speaks, but this no longer inhibits him from communicating effectively.

> *Remember what you've learned so far:*
> * *Fear and anxiety are minimized when we work at being ourselves rather than trying to be someone else.Improving our inherent strengths increases our level of confidence, thus reducing our level of fear.*

> • *Simplifying the structure of our content makes what we have to say much easier for listeners to grasp and absorb.*
> • *Knowing our desired outcome helps keep our communication focused (more on this later).*

A Helpful Paradigm Shift

Before leaving the topic of fear, allow me to share one more piece of advice that involves the matter of focus. Often, novice speakers become overly obsessed with themselves—how they will look, what they will sound like, will they forget something, etc. By thinking constantly about how they are perceived by others, they focus too much on themselves and not enough on their message. Changing this kind of thinking requires a fundamental paradigm shift, and making this shift can help decrease fear and minimize anxiety. The key is learning to shift the focus off yourself and more onto your message. Instead of obsessing about "you," shift your attention back on your preparation and presentation. Spend your time and effort researching your subject, rather than being overly fixated on yourself.

Experienced public speakers focus more on what is to be said than on the one saying it. In other words, the message must take precedence over concerns about the messenger. The following story illustrates my point.

Years ago an unwed teenage girl got pregnant. After considering all the options available to her, she decided to have the baby. For many reasons, she soon came to realize that she was not prepared to raise an infant. For the sake of the child, she decided to offer her baby up for adoption. In time, she found a couple that could not have a child, yet desperately wanted one. She carried the baby to full-term and tearfully handed over the newborn girl to the couple adopting her. Obviously, this was a gut-wrenching and painful experience for this young birth mom.

The adoption was open, meaning that the birth mom had the opportunity periodically to see her child. Although great in some ways, the open adoption made her life a lot more complicated, primarily because the visits were always bittersweet. The periodic reunions were wonderful, but the parting was excruciatingly difficult. Then in her early twenties, something began to stir within her. Although untrained and fearful at the thought of standing in front of a crowd, she felt compelled to tell other teenage girls about her difficult struggles. Her goal was to discourage other young girls from having premarital sex that could result in an unwanted or unplanned pregnancy. Passion and the vital nature of her message propelled her forward as she gallantly pressed through the acute anxiety that almost all novice speakers experience. By doing so, she demonstrated courage under fire. For a season, she stood before hundreds of teenagers telling her story. Although some took exception to her message, no one could argue about her sincerity. Over the years, this young woman has become a gifted presenter.

Remember, unless we allow it, fear and anxiety cannot stop us from sharing our message. This courageous woman proves this point every time she speaks. We will never know how many teenagers have avoided peril and pain because of her message, but, my guess is that there are many. No matter the number, I am so proud of her because she happens to be my daughter, Brandi.

Questions to Consider:
- *What are my strengths as a public speaker?*
- *What is my biggest challenge as a public speaker?*
- *What subject(s) am I most passionate about?*
- *Do I tend to focus more on my message or myself?*

CHAPTER TWO

Four Vital Questions

"SOMETIMES QUESTIONS ARE MORE
IMPORTANT THAN ANSWERS."
– Nancy Willard

M ost books contain a key chapter, and this is it. *If
you read and put into practice the principles included
here, you will definitely improve as a communicator.*
There are many questions a presenter can ask before speaking, but the following four are vital.

Question One:
To whom am I speaking?

The first question a presenter must answer involves the listening audience. The composition of a group influences what and how one prepares. Determining the makeup of an audience involves certain considerations that can be broken down into two categories: Demographics and Psychographics. "Demographics" help us define "age cells," while "Psychographics" inform us about "type cells."

Demographics. Initially, it is helpful to determine the demographic composite of the audience. We start by determining the average age of the crowd. Are there children?

If so, what age? If they are teenagers, are they young teens (13–16) or older teens (17–19)? If we find they are young adults, are they 18–24, 25–34, etc.? Now let me explain why this demographic analysis is so important.

The age of an audience influences the type of language, examples, and illustrations presenters use. For example, if I were talking to a group of young adults 18–24 years old about recent changes in the music industry, it would be more effective to drop names such as "Daughtry" and "Green Day" than "Chicago" and "The Beach Boys." Talking about the former would help me sound relevant and credible, while using the latter would date me and make me sound out of touch.

The key is to know the demographic makeup of your listening audience. Some audiences are demographically narrow in scope, but most are not. Generally, you will find that audiences are comprised of mixed age groups, and knowing this will help you tailor your examples and illustrations to impact the larger segments within the group.

Psychographics. Determining the psychographic profile of the audience is imperative as well. As previously stated, psychographics refers to "type cells," and all audiences are comprised of them. These cells inform us of the audience's inclinations and preferences, which is helpful information when addressing a group. Below is a short list of potential "types" you might find in a particular audience:

- Males or females
- Blue-collar workers or professionals
- Senior-level or junior-level managers
- Managers or employees

- Post-grad students or undergrad students
- Wine drinkers or beer drinkers
- Conservatives or Liberals
- Religious or non-religious individuals
- Doctors or lawyers
- Teachers or students
- Early adapters or late adopters
- Animal lovers or hunters

Suffice it to say that the age and type of people in any given audience will greatly impact the way you prepare to speak to them. But while the audience's profile will influence your method, it must never compromise or cause you to water-down your message. Instead, the core message simply needs to be packaged in terms relative to the audience at hand. Consequently, it is highly beneficial to know everything you can about the demographic and psychographic nature of the audience you will be addressing.

> *"A well prepared speech given to the wrong audience can have the same effect as a poorly prepared speech given to the correct audience. They both can fail terribly."*
> — Lenny Laskowski

Question Two:
How much time do I have to speak?

Suppose someone asked you to do a presentation on "The History of NASA's Space Program." Do you think the approach and content would be impacted by the length of time they gave you to speak? Of course it would. That is why knowing your allotted time upfront is so helpful. In many ways, the allotment time will inform you about how to approach your subject.

Coaching presenters involves helping them use their allotted time wisely. It is extremely difficult to prepare when the aforementioned question about time is unanswered. Take Phil, as an example. For a presentation at work, he was supposed to talk about a budget proposal to twenty senior-level managers. When I asked how much time he had been given to speak, he said, "between ten and twenty minutes." Obviously, there is a huge difference between talking for ten minutes and speaking for twenty. In the end, he realized he did not actually know how much time he had to talk. His assumption of ten to twenty minutes was based on prior years' presentations. When he circled back and asked his boss, he was told that the meeting agenda was packed, and he had, in fact, only seven minutes. As a result, this new-found information caused him to rethink the way he prepared his presentation.

Knowing the amount of time you have to speak is essential, but so is sticking to that time. Quite often presenters, to their own peril, violate the guidelines they are given. They decide that what they have to say is more important than the allotted time the host has given them. Good presenters figure out how to say what they want to say in the time provided. Presenters must learn that twenty minutes means twenty minutes, not twenty-five or thirty minutes. With few exceptions, it is highly inappropriate to talk longer than the time allotted. Presenters who fail to heed this advice are not likely to be invited back.

Some speakers who use the manuscript method (See Chapter 5) learn to measure their words in terms of time. For example, they read copy for five minutes, count the number of words they've read, and then divide by five to see how many words they normally speak in a minute. Once they have that number, they simply multiply the number of words they speak in a minute by the number of minutes they have been given to speak, and then write their speech accordingly.

Of course you may need to allow a little time for ad-libbing, dramatic pauses, and perhaps occasional clapping when you say something exciting, but this "formula" should help you craft a well-written talk that will fit neatly into the time frame you've been given. This is particularly important if you're giving a keynote morning or luncheon talk that will be followed by scheduled workshops or seminars.

Perhaps you have heard about the little boy sitting next to his dad at a political rally. At the beginning of his speech, the candidate took off his watch and placed it on the lectern that held his notes. The little boy turned to his dad and asked, "Dad, what does it mean when the speaker takes off his watch and puts it on the stand?" Dad turned to his young son, shook his head, and said, "Son, it means nothing, absolutely nothing!" Let this never be said about you.

Question Three:
What subject will I be addressing?

This may sound like an elementary question, but you would be surprised how many speakers try to prepare a talk before clearly defining their subject. Often, a presenter can give you a general idea of their topic, but not a specific one; it is this absence of a clearly defined subject that is the root cause of many subsequent problems. Here are just two. First, a fuzzy subject makes doing research difficult and, therefore, much more time consuming. Second, it creates confusion when you are trying to determine the goal of your presentation. Developing a clearly defined subject is so important that Chapter 3 is devoted entirely to this topic. For now, suffice it to say that the sooner you know the subject of your talk, the better.

Once you decide on a subject, make sure you can say it in simple terms. Speakers should be able to articulate clearly the reason for their talk in just a few words. Below are some pithy titles that leave little need for explanation. They pack a punch and make the subject matter clear to the casual observer:

- *How to Sell Sports Tickets on the Internet*
- *Three Missteps that Will Get You Fired*
- *Keys to Survival on the Battlefield*
- *Why Forgiving Can Extend Your Life*
- *What Not to Put in This Year's Budget*
- *The Top Four Reasons Businesses Fail*
- *The Attitudes that Will Get You Promoted*
- *The Best Way to Save Money on Hotels*

- *Why Worrying is Dangerous*
- *Three Vacation Destinations You Will Not Forget*

Now suppose you got a bonus at work and decided to take a well-deserved vacation. While thumbing through the local newspaper, you notice an advertisement promoting a seminar titled "Three Vacation Destinations You Will Not Forget." The day of the event you show up ready to hear about these must-see destinations, but at the end of the forty-minute talk, you realize the presenter has talked about everything except what you came to hear. You walk away feeling like the seminar's advertised title was a gross misrepresentation. This kind of thing happens more than you might think. Sadly, even when some presenters have a clear theme, they refuse to stick to it. They get sidetracked and lose focus on the subject at hand. Speakers who are guilty of this error damage their reputations and disappoint their audiences.

> If you publicize that you will be speaking about "The Meaning of Easter," don't talk about Santa Claus.

It is essential that we know what we have come to say, and that we do our best to say it. The more we deviate from the central theme, the more we dilute the subject. Perhaps you have heard it said, "If there is a mist on the podium, there is fog in the seats." In other words, a little ambiguity on the presenter's part can grow into mass confusion by the time it reaches the audience. *Listening audiences depend on presenters to be true to the title and subject they advertise. Failure to do so violates the listener's trust.* (The importance of "Identifying the Subject" and related matters is discussed at length in the next chapter.)

Question Four:
What is my desired outcome?

This question will be fully addressed in Chapter 4, but it is useful to touch upon it here as well. If you are preparing to speak, you have to ask WHY. What do you hope to accomplish? What do you want your audience to do at the end of your talk? Is it your goal that they do a particular thing, change an attitude or behavior, make a decision, take a step, join a cause, etc.? At the outset, it is imperative to decide on the end goal of your talk because knowing your "desired outcome" will clarify what you are trying to achieve and make your talk "purpose-centered." It will also ensure that all the elements of the talk dovetail together to support your intended outcome. Without a clear destination, we are sure to get sidetracked or even lost somewhere on the journey from preparation to delivery.

Suppose I told you I was going on a trip. What's the first question that comes to mind? For most it will be, "where are you going?" The same is true when it comes to preparing a talk. Once you evaluate your audience, understand how much time you have to speak, and determine your subject, then you are ready to start thinking about your desired outcome (goal). Again, what do you want your audience to do with what you are saying?

> *Establishing a desired outcome up front is much like choosing a target at the shooting range. You now have something to aim at. Without a clearly defined target, you are apt to waste your ammo.*
>
> *During your time of preparation, ask yourself these*

44

> *questions: If I could wave a magic wand, what would I like to see happen at the end of my talk? How would I like my audience to respond? Specifically, what would I like them to do?*

Those who read the last chapter know I fought in the Viet Nam War. One of the first people I saw when I returned home from the war zone was my older brother. At that time, he was a peace activist who was adamantly against the war in which I had fought. The first words out of his mouth were, "How many babies did you kill?" Not, "Welcome home! I'm glad you survived," but rather, "How many babies did you kill?"

His question wounded my war-weary soul. As hard as I tried, I could not totally forgive him. That is until I heard a stirring message on forgiveness. Believe me, I have heard plenty of talks on forgiveness, but not one like this. The speaker quoted Bible verses supporting his message, and he helped me understand the difference between forgetting and forgiving. Most importantly, he challenged us to pick a specific person and put into practice what we had learned (his desired outcome). Of course the first person that came to mind was my older brother.

It was not long after that we reconnected. We had not seen each other for quite some time, and now it was as if we had been providentially reunited. For some reason, we decided to go to the movies. I can count on one hand the number of times I have gone to the movies with my older brother. Of all the available movies, we went to see "Platoon," a movie about the war in Viet Nam. During one of the film's most intense battle scenes, I felt his hand gently touch mine. I do not recall him saying a word, but he didn't need to. I saw the request reflected in his eyes; eyes that asked me to forgive him for what he had said. In that moment, I knew I had to make a choice, one I would live with for the rest of my life. I chose to forgive him.

I am convinced God played a big role in softening my wounded heart. And I also know He used the man who spoke on forgiveness. That speaker prodded me to act on what I had learned. His goal was to get his audience to choose a person they needed to forgive, a person they had resented. His ultimate purpose was to transform his audience by challenging them to embrace forgiveness instead of resentment. I am happy to say that his desired outcome was realized in me.

CHAPTER THREE

Identifying the Subject

> "GRASP THE SUBJECT, THE
> WORDS WILL FOLLOW."
> –Cato The Elder

Every talk or presentation needs a subject—a *single* subject that will be the core theme of your presentation. The Cambridge Advanced Learning Dictionary defines "subject" as being, "The area of study–the thing which is being discussed, considered, or studied." Often, the term "subject" is referred to as the topic, main thought, central idea, key proposition, theme, or thesis statement. Building your talk on a singular subject will keep it focused and specific.

Generally, experienced presenters are free to select their own subject, but not always. Sometimes their topic is selected for them. Whether it is chosen or given, you must ensure that you stick to a single subject, because multiple subjects make for confusing and hard-to-follow presentations. Trying to speak on two subjects is like riding two skateboards downhill at the same time. Let's try it. Go and find a nice paved hill. Put the skateboards down on the ground side by side and place one foot on each of them. Now try keeping your balance as you ride down the hill.

How was that for you? Should I call an ambulance? Structuring a talk with more than one subject is as foolish as this silly example. We go this way and that way, pursuing one subject, and then the other. In the end, we do the "splits" and fail to do justice to either subject. Make the commitment to restrict yourself to one key topic per talk. Certainly, you can talk about various aspects of that subject, but stick to the primary topic. This advice will serve you well.

As previously mentioned, you may be asked to pick a subject for your presentation or be given a predetermined one. Over time you will certainly experience both situations. In my case, about eighty percent of the time I choose my own topic. Because you will undoubtedly encounter each situation, it is useful to talk about both of them.

> *Sometimes you choose your subject and sometimes your subject chooses you.*

When you are allowed to pick your own subject, your assignment may be a bit easier because you get to choose a subject you know and care something about. Conversely, it can be a bit more difficult as well because you have so many possible options from which to choose. Finding what topic to land on can be frustrating and quite time-consuming, but this problem is not as difficult to solve as you might think.

Remember the four vital questions discussed in Chapter 2? Well there is a reason we started there. Once you have answered the first question, you have a keen understanding about the demographic and psychographic nature of your audience. Then by answering the second question, you know how much time you have to speak. This important information goes a long way in helping you answer question three, "What subject will I be addressing?"

Knowing your audience furthers your understanding of their interests and needs. It helps you scratch them where they itch. This is why answering vital questions 1 and 2 is so important before you begin honing in on a subject. *Time spent studying your audience is never wasted.*

Generally, the best talks come from presenters who speak on topics that resonate with their own values. These devoted orators talk about subjects that matter to them deeply. They speak with power and passion because they believe so strongly in what they are saying.

When you have the freedom to pick your topic, you have a chance to talk about what matters to you. The challenge here is convincing your audience that the value(s) you are speaking about ought to matter to them as well. Many classic talks, speeches, sermons, and presentations are deemed great not because they echo the sentiments of the day, but because they stimulate listeners to think and act differently. These speakers do this by encouraging their audience to reexamine what they believe, what they value, and where to invest their time.

Years ago I was privileged to attend a dinner party given in honor of astronaut Jim Irwin. Part of the evening's program included a talk by Jim, who spoke on "The Power of Encouragement." It was a talk I'll never forget because it changed the way I feel and think about encouragement.

Jim began his talk by recalling a childhood incident that changed his life. One evening he and his mother were out on their front porch. (I seem to recall him saying that he was young enough then to be sitting on his mother's lap.) The night sky was clear and brilliantly dotted with stars. Suddenly, Jim looked at his mom and then once again up at the sky. After a short pause he said, "Mom, someday I'm going to walk on the moon."

Jim's mom was also at the dinner that night, so when Jim said this, I glanced over at her. She was nodding her head in agreement, and the cutest smile you can imagine come over her aged face as she was surely remembering his outlandish childish statement that night. You see, at that point, no one had ever walked on the moon, so what was a mother to say?

As Jim continued his story back on the porch, he said he stared at his mom and waited for her response. It was one of those pregnant pauses that are noisy with thought. Finally, Jim's mom said, "Son, maybe someday you *will* walk on the moon," and those encouraging words set the course for the rest of that little boy's life.

On July 26, 1971 at 9:34 a.m., Colonel Jim Irwin, commander of Apollo 15 set off for the moon with his crew. This was NASA's fourth manned lunar expedition. Four days later, on July 30, the lunar module "Falcon" landed on the moon's surface. During that visit Jim Irwin fulfilled his childhood dream and walked on the moon.

Jim's inspirational talk celebrated the power and impact of his mother's encouragement. It also changed the way I think about and value encouragement. Since then, I have worked hard to be an encourager. I doubt that I will ever encourage a moonwalk, but perhaps someone reading this story just might come to believe they, too, can do something that others say is impossible. That is good enough for me.

Jim Irwin focused on a single subject that night, speaking for only about twenty minutes. But he beamed with passion and talked about a subject that mattered to him deeply. As a result, he touched his audience in a life-changing way.

Celebrate the opportunity to choose your own topic when you get the chance to do so. Study your audience and tap into your knowledge base, values, experience, and passions. This alone can help you find the subject for your presentation much quicker than you think.

> *Consider these things when choosing a subject:*
> * *The subject should be of interest and value to your audience.*
> * *The subject should be within your knowledge base. (If it is not, extensive research will be a must.)*
> * *The subject should evoke a sense of passion in you.*
> * *The subject should be age- and audience-appropriate.*

Seek Clarity

Now it's time to discuss a different scenario. Unlike our previous example, this time you are being told what subject to speak on. In some ways this will be easier, but in others, a bit harder. Easier because you won't need to spend time searching for a subject; harder because, depending on your knowledge base, you might need to spend a good deal of time researching the topic.

When given a subject to speak on, make sure you ask for clarification if you need it. For example, suppose you are asked to speak about "How New York City has changed since 9/11." A few clarifying questions would be in order, such as: Do you want me to talk about changes related to the people's mentality? Changes in way the city deals with security? Changes that have taken place in the economy? Or, would you prefer I talk about some other type of change?

Failure to ask the right kinds of questions can result in an off-target presentation and a disappointed host and audience. I learned this lesson the hard way many years ago when the vice-president of human resources asked me to speak to a small group of leaders at a Silicon Valley high-tech company. He assigned me the topic of "executive coaching," which I thought was a slam-dunk inasmuch as I owned a senior-level executive consulting company. He was busy and very harried the day he gave me the assignment. As a result, we did not have much time to talk. So, I took the assignment and made some assumptions about the subject, assumptions I later regretted. Instead of picking up the phone and seeking clarification, I assumed I understood what he wanted me to do. I was so *wrong*.

The morning of the engagement I walked into the conference room and received a warm greeting from the participants. After a few preliminaries, I began my talk. Within minutes, it was obvious something was wrong. The group became more and more fidgety. They began looking more at one another than at me. After a few painful minutes, the VP interrupted me. To make a long story short, my assumptions about what I thought he wanted were wrong. Although I spoke on a related subject, it was not the one he

52

intended or wanted. As a result, I lost the account. All in all, it was one of the most embarrassing and expensive lessons of my speaking career.

Remember earlier when I talked about learning by wisdom or consequences? Let my consequences teach you a bit of wisdom. In this regard, please don't make the same mistake. Ensure that you are clear on your assignment. Be certain you understand specifically what you are being asked to speak about.

Do Your Research

Once you are sure you know your subject, research it thoroughly. This is easy with tools like the Internet. Basic searches on words and subjects will net you a great deal of information. For example, a keyword search for "speech topics" on Google or your favorite search engine will put a plethora of potential subjects instantly at your fingertips.

A Word on Titles

A presentation is enhanced and supported by a clear and concise title. That title should succinctly describe the nature of what will be said and leave no questions about your subject. A good title will usually reveal how you plan on approaching the subject. Here is a short list of topic titles that are clear and concise:

How to Find a Good Pediatrician
Three Reasons Why I Want to be Your Governor

Where to Find the Best Oranges in Florida
Four Reasons People are Buying the iPad
Tips for Treating a Bee Sting
Why the Medical Industry is Losing Nurses
Signs That It's Time for a Career Change
How to Write a Children's Book
Why We Go to Church on Sunday

Teaching Methods

After you figure out what you want to say, you need to decide how you want to say it—specifically, which instructional method you will use to present your material. (Some refer to this as "unpacking the subject.") It is beneficial for aspiring speakers to listen to speeches, presentations, and talks of all kinds for examples on the approaches being used by other presenters. There are different ways of teaching a subject, but for our purposes here only two will be discussed: the "deductive" method and the "inductive" method. Both are highly effective but very different in the manner in which messages are conveyed.

> **Deductive Method**. The "deductive" method is a standard teaching model that looks like this: Principle Stated → Examples Given → Proof in Practice.
>
> A deductive talk on worry could be structured this way:
>
> **Title:** The Truth About Worry

Principle Stated: Worry can kill you!

Examples Given: Statistics and supportive material showing the health risks associated with worry.

Proof in Practice: Worry can kill you! Stories of people suffering or dying from stress-related illnesses; suggestions designed to help listeners overcome worry.

This is a simple example of using the deductive approach to teach on the subject of "worry." The biggest problem with this method is that it tends to eliminate the element of surprise and most of the positive tension in the talk. When the principle is stated up front, listeners often think they already know what is going to be said. Unfortunately, this means the presenter has to work even harder to keep their interest and attention. Nonetheless, the deductive method is a powerful way to state your case and use the rest of your talk proving it.

Inductive Method. The "inductive" method is a quite different teaching approach. You might say it is somewhat of a reverse of the deductive method. The inductive method looks like this: Examples Given → Proof in Practice → Principle Stated.

An inductive talk on worry might be structured this way:

Title: What Most People Don't Know About Worry

Examples Given: Stories of people dying or suffering from stress related illnesses.

Proof in Practice: Statistics cited about health risks associated with worry.

Principle Stated: The most important thing you need to know about worry is "Worry can kill you!"

The inductive approach allows the presenter to build to a climax, with the principal supposition being held in tension until the latter part of the message. This method captivates listeners by using examples and illustrations that hold their attention until the key principle is stated at or near the end of the talk.

Unlike the deductive method, the inductive method (if done well) holds the listener's attention because the key point is not stated up front. This can be a very powerful and effective method when used properly.

Generally, my preference is the inductive method of teaching because people like surprise endings. However, many great teachers prefer the deductive approach. In the end, gifted teachers do not let a method determine their approach. They analyze their audience and subject and evaluate the best way to achieve their desired outcome.

A Warning about Plagiarism

In today's Information Age, plagiarism is rampant. Because it is a great temptation for both speakers and writers to plagiarize the work of others, I must conclude this chapter with a cautionary note on this topic. Believe me when I say that falling prey to this temptation will cost you big time. Executives, professionals, and students are summarily dismissed many times because of plagiarism. *Do not do it! It is not worth it.* Better to be an average presenter who is authentic, than a great speaker or writer who is a fraud.

I am reminded of the wonderful story in a book titled *The Empty Pot* by Demi (Henry Holt, 1996). (Children and adults are sure to enjoy this wonderfully illustrated little book, and I highly recommend its purchase.) The story, which has a strong moral message, is about a little boy in China named Ping who had a green thumb and a gift for growing beautiful flowers. When the Kingdom's Emperor, who also loved flowers, decided it was time to find a successor to the throne, he arranged a test whereby he gave many children in the Kingdom flower seeds saying that the child who grew the most beautiful flowers from these seeds would be named the new Emperor.

Despite many months of trying first one thing and then another to get the seeds to grow, Ping was unsuccessful and heartbroken when nothing happened. At year's end, when all the children returned to the palace with pots filled with beautiful flowers grown from seeds they had obtained elsewhere, Ping went with his empty pot, assured by his father that he had done the best he could.

As it turned out, the Emperor had tricked the children, giving them seeds that had been cooked. When they wouldn't grow all the children, except Ping, substituted different seeds that filled their pots with beautiful flowers. But the Emperor chose Ping as his successor because he admired his courage to come to him with the truth and an empty pot.

Authenticity is one mark of good character, and this story is a reminder to presenters to consider issues of character as well as competence. Plagiarism negates authenticity and reveals flawed character. It also puts us in great jeopardy. So learn the lesson Ping's story teaches us, that it is better to show up with an empty pot than to arrive with a pot full of flowers you did not grow.

CHAPTER FOUR

Beginning at the End

"WITHOUT GOALS, AND PLANS TO REACH
THEM, YOU ARE LIKE A SHIP THAT HAS SET
SAIL WITH NO DESTINATION."
–Fitzhugh Dodson

Furthering the information in Chapter 2 about the importance of having a "desired outcome," this chapter explores that topic in detail. Once you choose a subject, you are ready to think about the goal of your talk. Many presenters wait far too long to think about their desired outcome, so once you know what you are going to talk about, it's time to consider what you hope to accomplish.

Beginning at the end will foster what might be called a "purpose-centered talk." However, this requires that you know your objective before you get too far into your preparation. Just as a train needs a destination and a track, so our talks need a purpose and a structure. The purpose determines our goal while the structure maps our course.

As a ten-year-old boy, I raised pigeons in the backyard of our small home in Daly City, California. I still remember building the pigeon coop and getting it ready for my first birds. When that day arrived, I discovered there was a lot to learn about pigeons, and I found out that there were different kinds of pigeons as well. Back then, I thought all pigeons were alike, but they aren't. After careful investigation, I chose two different kinds of pigeons to take home. One breed was called "rollers," the other "homers." Rollers are trick pigeons that actually do tumbles in the air, while homers are unique birds that can be trained to find their way home, even from great distances.

In time, the homing pigeons won me over. They were fascinating creatures. The pigeon coop I built had a little opening that served as a door that was simply a bent-wire coat hanger. The door was designed so the birds could go in the coop but not come out of it.

The homing pigeons were trained in an interesting way. A few times a day, I held the pigeons outside the cage and then gently nudged them back into it through the little one-way door. After doing this repeatedly for a few days, I would take a pigeon out of the coop, walk a few yards away and let it go. This was a great exercise in faith for a little boy. Part of me wondered if they might not just fly away and never return. Actually, the pigeons would fly off for a while. Yet, eventually to my delight, they would return to the small perch that sat in front of the coat hanger door. After awhile, they would walk through the little door into the cage just the way they had been trained. In time, I could take them miles away, let them go, and they would miraculously return home every time.

Homing pigeons and presenters have this in common: they both need to learn where home is before they can be released. The pigeon's home is a coop. The presenter's home is a predetermined desired outcome, and it is this well thought-out objective that makes the presentation "purpose-centered."

Early on, presenters must determine exactly how they want to finish by deciding what they hope their audience will do in response to their talk. That is why it is so critical that you begin with your focus on the end. Without a clearly defined objective up front, you are likely to stray off course. It is no fun to climb the ladder and then realize it is leaning against the wrong wall.

Know What You Want To Happen

Suppose you were running for a public office. And let's say you were slated to give a fifteen-minute speech. After answering three of the four questions described in Chapter 2, you should be ready to decide on your desired outcome. Is it to give a good speech? (That may be good, but it is not best.) Is your goal to sell your particular political ideology? (Of course, but again, while that may be on target, it's not a bull's-eye.)

Ultimately, your real objective here would be "to get votes." Once you have arrived at this conclusion, it becomes your home base, your destination, your driving purpose, your desired outcome. Knowing your true goal will help you stay focused on what you need to say and what you eventually want your audience to do—in this case, get them to vote for you.

Speaking without a purpose is pointless. It is like running a race without a finish line. On the other hand, when you have taken the time to pinpoint your purpose, your whole talk will reflect it. Your introduction, movements (more on this later), illustrations, application(s), and conclusion will all support this end goal.

What Does "A Win" Look Like?

"Beginning at the end," means asking two fundamental questions from the start. First, what do I want my listeners to do at the conclusion of my talk? Second, what does "a win" look like? Answering these questions will help define and clarify your purpose.

Years ago, I managed a radio station in Jacksonville, Florida called WIVY, also known as Y103. For most of my years in the radio business, I was a "turn-around specialist." Corporations hired me to rejuvenate stations with sagging ratings and increase their bottom-line profits.

When I arrived in Jacksonville, I remember addressing the station's employees about my commitment to winning. My short-term goal was to become the top rated radio station in Jacksonville. My long-term goal was to stay there. To achieve this lofty aim, a lot of change was necessary that threatened the status quo. When I spoke to the station's employees, my desired outcome was to promote the need for alignment and to rekindle their passion to win. To achieve my desired outcome, I had to create a tipping point. Each employee had a decision to make. The choice was simple: align with the new vision, or choose not to, in which case I would assist them in finding a job elsewhere. Over the next couple of weeks my talk did exactly what I intended. Those inspired by my vision and leadership began displaying new levels of passion, commitment, and productivity. Conversely, those unimpressed and uninspired faded away as quickly as a winter spray tan. Within a year and a half, WIVY FM became the top-rated radio station in Jacksonville by a landslide. How? It all started with a purpose-centered talk that inspired a group of people to believe that their radio station could be the best in town. This is a good example of what "a win" looks like.

Think about an upcoming talk you intend to give, or one you have already given. Did you begin at the end? Did you have a clearly defined purpose? If the answer is yes, congratulations! If not, how did things go? Although some people intuitively know how to salvage a talk without a desired outcome, it is far from the optimal approach. Defining your purpose will make you

> *Beginning at the end means your eyes are always on the predetermined prize. Radio managers fix their sights on ratings and profits, archers aim at a target and a bull's-eye, and good speakers focus on a specific goal and a predetermined outcome.*

a better presenter and enhance your ability to impact your audience in a predetermined way. Your presentations will be easier to follow, and you will be much clearer about your stated expectations. In other words, developing a purpose-centered method of speaking will make you a more focused and effective communicator.

A great example of a presenter that knows how to "begin at the end" is television's favorite doctor, Mehmet Oz, host of the Emmy Award-winning "Dr. Oz Show." Weekdays, millions of television viewers tune in to Dr. Oz. to watch his informative TV show that promotes the benefits of healthy living. Dr. Oz is both a proponent of healthy living and a master at purposeful presentations.

Recently, I watched a show about the liver. I normally

would have changed the channel when I heard the subject, but I was captivated by his compelling introduction and found myself gripped by his purpose-centered presentation. I could hardly believe I was actually watching a show about the liver. He began by describing the functions of a healthy liver, the body's largest organ (except for skin). He talked about the liver performing a number of vital functions, including metabolizing food and drugs, removing toxins from the bloodstream, storing vitamins and minerals, producing proteins that help the blood clot, and producing bile that helps digest food and nutrients.

Doctor Oz informed the audience that the liver is about the size of football. He verified his assertion by showing viewers an actual detached liver, one that had obviously been mistreated. It was not pretty. Within minutes, the audience was chomping at the bit (and so was I) to know how to avoid ending up with a diseased or damaged liver.

By now, we were glued to our sets and ready to receive whatever advice Dr. Oz had to offer. Frankly, before the show, I had not given two seconds to thinking about my liver. Now I was keenly aware of this vital body part and my need to treat it with care. Dr. Oz's presentation caused me to quit doing shots of tequila the very next day. Just kidding! Seriously, his presentation did cause me to reexamine my food and beverage intake and their impact on this vital organ.

Doctor Oz knew the purpose of his presentation from the outset. He skillfully helped his audience understand why they needed to embrace his recommendations and provided them with practical tips for keeping the liver healthy and functioning properly. When it comes to an example of quality presentations, Dr. Oz rocks. Check him out. I'm sure you will discover, as I did, that he has a lot to teach us about both healthy living and purposeful presentations.

By now, I am confident that you understand the significance of beginning at the end. Incorporating this practice into your preparations will enhance your effectiveness and keep your train on the tracks. Like the homing pigeon, you will never get lost because you know the way home. Craft your talks to be purpose-centered, then make sure your supporting elements do just that . . . support your desired outcome.

Speech Styles

Assuming you have answered the four questions discussed in Chapter 2, you now know the makeup of your audience, how much time you have to speak, your subject, and your predetermined desired outcome. Now let's look at another tool that will help you reach your predetermined goal.

When you prepare your talks, it is imperative that you choose a "speech style" that supports your proposed goal. This is accomplished by matching the style of your talk with your intended outcome. Below is a list of the most prominent speech styles along with their associate goals:

Type of Speech	*Goal*
Motivational	Call to Action
Demonstration	Show how to
Informational	Increase knowledge

Type of Speech	Goal
Inspirational	Encourage
Opinion	Convince
Rebuttal	Repudiate
Acceptance	Acknowledge
Tribute	Celebrate
Sermon	Transform

The style of talk you choose is largely influenced by your desired outcome. If you want to encourage your listeners to "do" something, a *motivational talk* is your best bet. If you want to "show" them how to do something, a *demonstration talk* is a wise choice. Should you want to convince your audience to adopt a specific viewpoint, a *persuasive talk* is the preferred method. You get the point, I'm sure. I recommend that you take time to study these and other presentation styles because this will equip you to be ready for whatever comes your way. The more tools you have in your bag, the better.

In the next chapter, our focus will be on talking about issues related to the message's structure.

CHAPTER FIVE

Hiding the Structure

Structure describes the underpinnings of a message and helps the presenter arrange the flow of the talk. All talks have a structure that shapes content. That structure can be poorly designed or even unintentional, but it is a structure nonetheless. Failing to pay careful attention to the organizational structure of a talk is a mistake because talks without an intentional structure often fall flat.

Suppose we go to the local mall and look in the window of a men's clothing store. Most likely, we will see suits on display. But they won't just be lying on the floor; they will be hanging on mannequins. Structure does for a message what a mannequin does for a suit: a mannequin gives a suit shape, and structure gives a speaker's message form.

The human body also illustrates this concept. It is hard to imagine a body without a skeleton. The skeleton gives our flesh something that shapes it. In like fashion, structure gives our message a form on which to hang its content. The skeleton is not meant to be on display, neither is your message's structure. Just as the skeleton is hidden behind our skin, so our structure should be veiled behind our message.

> **Basic Structural Methods:**
> - The Manuscript Method
> - The Outline Method
> - The Keyword Outline Method
> - The Movement Method

The structure we choose depends largely on the content being conveyed and the comfort level of the presenter. Generally, the more knowledgeable and comfortable a presenter is, the looser the structure can be. Of course, there are exceptions that will be addressed shortly. For now, it is beneficial for speakers to know there are a variety of different ways to structure a talk. Most speakers rely on one of the following methods to organize their content.

The Manuscript Method

Structure varies depending on the message and the messenger. Some speakers like to use the "manuscript method;" in which they write out their message word for word, and leave nothing to chance. These presenters have something specific to say, and they do not want any errors or omissions. Although this method has distinct advantages, it also comes with some inherent risks.

On the positive side of the ledger, using a manuscript allows presenters to fine-tune their words and meticulously craft their sentences. Hopefully, nothing they have prepared is missed or muffed. Nonetheless, I do not recommend this approach for most speakers, and here's why. The best users of this method can speak without appearing to be reading from their script, thus keeping their skeleton hidden.

However, this takes a lot of practice and experience. Conversely, many speakers who use this method end up showing too much skeleton.

Using a manuscript is risky for many speakers because they end up paying more attention to the page than the people, and this makes connecting with the audience much more difficult. Failing to connect with the audience derails many presentations. On the other hand, connecting with listeners helps foster a friendlier and more forgiving speaking environment.

Tiger Woods is arguably the best golfer that ever lived. There is an old saying, "The bigger they are, the harder they fall," and Tiger took a big tumble when news surfaced of his involvement in several extramarital affairs. Pursuant to his very publicized fall, Tiger enlisted professional help and enrolled in a forty-five day treatment program designed to help him begin a process of recovery. Needing to resurrect his tarnished image, he decided to hold an invitation-only press conference on February 19, 2010 that was broadcast live on ESPN. This gathering was intended to be a public platform for Mr. Woods to speak about personal and professional issues. I watched the event not only to hear what Tiger had to say, but to see how he would come across to the listening and viewing public. Understandably, he chose to speak from a manuscript. He knew every word spoken would be sliced and diced. The manuscript allowed him to choose his words carefully. There was no room for chance. Every word was calculated and every sentence crafted to convey exactly what Tiger wanted to say.

At the end of his talk, which might be better characterized as a long statement, he said what he planned to say.

However, there was a problem. The manuscript had served him in one way, but failed him in another. The next day, the headline in the *San Jose Mercury* at the bottom of the sports page read, "Woods' scripted apology perfectly awkward." The article went on to say, "He stayed too on the script, maybe not in the eyes of public-relation's advisers but definitely for the average fan. [. . .] From the start, it was as awkward to watch as it must have been painfully uncomfortable for him to deliver. It looked too staged, too phony, like a *Saturday Night Live* skit with satin-blue curtains, a malfunctioning camera, and a lonely guy delivering an informercial-esque monologue."[3]

In watching Tiger speak, it was evident he was not connecting with his audience. The manuscript he used dominated his attention. He continually looked down instead of out. Only a few times did he speak to his listeners and not at them. His approach resulted in many feeling that he was insincere about what he said.

Whether Tiger was sincere or not is unimportant for our purposes. I do not know him nor do I choose to judge him. However, we can see from this event how a manuscript can get between a speaker and the audience. Let me reiterate that I understand why Tiger chose to use a manuscript. In essence, he needed to be precise and did not want extra words diluting his message. Yet, in my opinion, and that of many others, the way he used his manuscript worked more to his detriment than to his advantage. So if you choose or need to use a manuscript, master the text. That way you can stay engaged with your audience while you talk. *It is a*

3 San Jose Mercury News, Sports pp. 1 and 3, Cam Inman, February 20, 2010.

mistake to neglect the people for the page. The audience needs to see your eyes, not the top of your head.

When all is said and done, if you must use a manuscript, by all means use it. However, if you do not need it, I encourage you to try an alternative structural method. Having said this, the manuscript method can be very useful, especially in more technical and scientific talks where facts and figures are plentiful and accuracy is essential. If you are in this kind of situation, try a manuscript. An alternative suggestion is to manuscript only the key segments of your talk, instead of the whole presentation. This will allow you to stay more engaged with your audience while remaining precise and accurate when that is essential.

The Outline Method

Another structural approach is the "outline method," which is very popular among presenters for a simple reason. Speakers find outlining a great tool for organizing their talks, but presenters who use the outline method must be careful not to sound like they are speaking from an outline. Remember that the talk's structure needs to be hidden. People do not talk or hold conversations in outline form. If they did, the discussions would probably sound very unnatural.

Using an outline demands that you pay careful attention to how you transition from one point to the next. Good transitions can make an outline sound seamless, while awkward transitions can make the flow of your presentation sound choppy. Poor transitions tend to highlight your structure and detract from your message. If you use an outline, just make sure you don't *sound* like you are using one.

The Keyword Outline Method

An offshoot of the outline method is the "keyword outline." This method does exactly what it says: creates an outline using keywords. These trigger words guide the speaker from one point or movement to the next. This approach allows a presenter to condense their outline to something as small as an index card or even smaller. Unlike the manuscript and full outline method, you won't have to worry about being a slave to your notes because you will have very few.

Speakers who use little or no notes have an advantage when it comes to connecting with the audience. However, they have a lot more to remember when it comes to content. Even so, this is a great technique when doing talks twenty minutes or under in length.

The first Tea Party Convention was held in Nashville, Tennessee in February 2010. At the gathering, keynote speaker Sarah Palin created quite a stir. It was not what she said that unleashed the storm, but what she did. She used a keyword outline. The controversy ensued because she wrote that keyword outline on the palm of her hand. Here are the actual keywords that she wrote on her hand:

Energy
Budget
Tax
Lift American Spirits

The incident became fodder for the news media and bloggers for days. They accused her of using a "cheat sheet" at the convention. Instead of using an index card or sheet of paper, Mrs. Palin chose to write her keywords on her hand. Now I ask you, what is the big deal? Regardless of your political leanings, the ruckus over this incident was much to do about nothing. What difference does it make if someone chooses to write their keywords on their hand, a piece of paper, or read them off of a teleprompter? I will applaud any presenter that can talk intelligently for several minutes using only four key words. Perhaps that is why Sarah Palin is known for connecting so well with her audiences. She is never tied to her notes.

Many gifted and experienced speakers use keyword outlines, but they are not for the faint of heart. Those who use them must know their material well. The keyword is the trigger, but there had better be a round in the barrel. This technique is a great way to learn to think on your feet, so you might make it a goal to speak with a keyword outline when you are presenting a short talk and grow from there.

Examples of basic speaking outlines are plentiful online. The following sites show various outlining models and may be helpful to some:

www.speech-topics-help.com/sample-persuasive-speech-outline.html

www.ismckenzie.com/outline-template-for-writing-a-speech

www.speakersuccessonline.com/63/create-speaking-outline

Examples of keyword outlines can be found here:

www.tpub.com/content/photography/14129/css/14129_166.htm

www.helium.com/items/1604721-how-to-create-a-key-word-outline

Practice Helps

Here is a great way to practice keyword talks in the privacy of your own room. Prepare a three-minute talk on "Why You Should Try My Favorite Restaurant." Your desired outcome is to get your listeners to go to your favorite restaurant and try a favorite meal. For this exercise do not worry about answering the four vital questions listed in Chapter 2. Simply spend 30 seconds highlighting why this is your favorite restaurant, 30 seconds talking about a succulent appetizer, one minute describing the perfect entrée, and 30 seconds talking about a killer dessert. Close the talk with a 30 second invitation for your audience to join you next week at the restaurant for a meal. If you have never done a keyword talk before, try it. It is fun! And yes, if need be, you can write your keywords on the palm of your hand:

Restaurant
Appetizer
Entrée
Dessert
Invitation

One final thought about keyword outlines. In 1990 gubernatorial candidate Diane Feinstein was caught during the California Debate for Governor using keyword notes that she had written on her hand. Unfortunately, this was against the debate rules, so make sure when you use a keyword outline that it is permitted. When acceptable, it can give you a big hand up!

The Movement Method

The methods described so far are effective ways of structuring a presentation. I have used each of them at one time or another, but most of the time I use a slightly different approach known as the "movement method." It is a modification of a concept I learned under the tutelage of Dr. Haddon Robinson. The movement method describes a series of thought units connected by a singular subject, and it is designed to achieve a specific desired outcome. In this modified outline model, the major thought units are called "movements."

This approach abandons the traditional outline method (I, II, III, A, B, C, 1, 2, 3) in favor of a less formal and more naturally flowing structure. This hybrid method tends to sound smoother and more conversational than the traditional outline method.

The movement method keeps the presenter from falling prey to "blankaphobia" (my word), which I define as a compulsion to fill in all the blanks of a traditional outline, whether or not one has something more to say. Some who use the outline method get stuck in this "catch twenty-two." Driven to fill in every space, Blankaphobics feel compelled to write something after every Roman numeral, capital letter, and number, etc. To them, the outline is the master not the servant. If there is an "A" and a "B," then there has to be a "C," even if they are not sure why they need one. This phobia can make for some awkward moments during presentations. Usually, it is fairly easy to identify where the real substance ends and the fluffy fill-ins begin.

You won't have this problem if you use the movement method of structuring your presentation. "Movements" are thought units that flow naturally toward a desired outcome. Each thought unit plays a key role in moving the audience ever closer to the message's intended application. There are no blanks to fill in, only the number of movements needed to realize the predetermined goal. The movement method helps presentations sound more conversational and less choppy because there are fewer awkward outline transitions. Finally, because of the limited number of notes associated with this method, speakers spend less time glancing at their notes and more time connecting with their audience.

Generally, I prefer the movement method because it is easier for listeners to follow and simpler when it comes to structuring. I rarely need more than a sheet or two of paper to lay out a talk. Allow me to illustrate how I might prepare and structure a short talk using a simple form of the "movement method."

Preliminary Information

Question one: *To whom am I speaking? I am speaking to a group of male professional managers 25 – 44 years old. They are college graduates making, $80,000 to $120,000 per year. They are interested in learning how to develop the character and competencies of people they manage. I am one of four speakers at this half-day seminar entitled, "The Value and Process of Executive Development."*

Question two: *How much time do I have to speak? I've been given fifteen minutes to talk and an additional half hour for questions and discussion.*

Question three: *What subject will I be addressing? I am the third speaker. The first two presenters are talking on the "value" of executive development. I am speaking about the "process" of executive development. My approach is inductive. My subject is "How to develop your direct reports."*

Question four: *What is my desired outcome? To ask managers to write out a personal developmental plan for themselves that they can use as a model to help develop others they manage. They will highlight two personal strengths they would like to develop, and two personal challenges they are committed to address. Participants will use S.M.A.R.T. goals to make sure their plans are realized. [4]*

Title: *Keys to Developing the People You Manage*

Talk Style: *Motivational (call to action)*

Introduction: *Story about a company continually losing promising executives because it lacks an employee development plan. Developing the people you manage will not only help them grow, but it will also improve the company's ability to retain quality employees.*

Transition: *What are the "keys" to developing my direct reports? We begin by "Modeling Development."*

---

4 Smart Goals – S = Specific, M = Measurable, A = Attainable, R = Realistic, T = Timely

Movement one (Key 1): Model it! - Demonstrate your commitment to executive development by working your own plan and sharing it with those you manage.

Illustration: Story of the manager who modeled transparency and established a culture of development.

Transition: Being open about your own development is a great start, but you must also "Promote Development." Let me tell you what that looks like:

Movement two (Key 2): Promote it! – Make executive development a priority. We do this by <u>teaching it</u>, <u>encouraging it</u>, and <u>discussing it</u> often (underline indicates subpoints within this movement).

Statistical Support: Statistical data that proves that team dynamics and productivity improved measurably following a leadership developmental workshop.

Transition: Modeling and promoting development are vital, but we must not neglect the third key, "Measuring Development."

Movement three (Key 3): Measure it! – Individual and team "developmental plans" must be monitored and measured against predetermined objectives.

Illustration: Story of a manager noticing incremental

growth in a recently hired employee resulting in an opportunity to encourage her.

Transition: *We now see the benefits of modeling, promoting, and measuring employee and team development. Yet, there is still one more key. We must "Celebrate Development."*

Movement four (Key 4): Celebrate it! *– Institute forums for recognizing and rewarding individual and team development and accomplishments.*

Illustration: *Humorous – Celebration gone awry - jumping into the pool before realizing my cell phone was in my bathing suit pocket.*

Review: *Remind audience of the four keys - Movements 1–4.*

Call for Action: *First, ask managers in attendance to write out a personal developmental plan using S.M.A.R.T. goals that they will share with their direct reports. Second, institute an employee developmental plan for each direct report within 90 days.*

Close: *Inspirational story of highly successful CEO who became a great leader because of a dedicated mid-level manager.*

Note: *The above example is illustrative. Generally, my notes are quite a bit shorter.*

> S.M.A.R.T. Goals
> S.M.A.R.T. goals are those that are Specific,
> Measurable, Attainable, Realistic, and Timely.

In wrapping up this chapter on structure, here are a few closing considerations:

- Structure must always serve and never master the presenter. If the structural approach you choose handcuffs you in any way or interferes with you connecting with the audience, try a different method.

- Limit structure whenever possible as long as it does not adversely impact the nature or flow of your content. Use as much structure as necessary, but no more. All talks need some structure but generally less than most presenters realize.

- Do not be afraid to rely on your recall. Condensing your notes will help you practice this. If you have a crutch, you will most likely use it. In the absence of one, you will limp a bit until you learn to walk.

As a novice speaker, I recall using a lot of notes. Over time, the length of my notes decreased. Using fewer notes was a bit risky, but with fewer notes my ability to think on my feet increased significantly, and so did my confidence. In the end, make it your ambition to depend more on your recall than on your notes. Try to utilize different structural methods. In time you will learn what method serves you best. And remember: whatever method you choose, make certain that it highlights the suit and not the mannequin.

CHAPTER 6

The Ninety-Second Rule

Before talking about the ninety-second rule, it might be helpful to do a bit of review. Earlier, I explained that building a talk begins by analyzing the audience and clarifying your assignment. At that time I highlighted "four vital questions" that help us in this regard:

Question One: *To whom am I speaking?*
Question Two: *How much time do I have to speak?*
Question Three: *What subject will I be addressing?*
Question Four: *What is my desired outcome?*

When we have answered these critical questions, we're ready for the next step in our process, which is refining our subject. Careful attention to this important detail ensures we have a "single" subject that clearly reflects what we want to say. In the discussion about "beginning at the end," the focus was on determining our "desired outcome" in advance. (At the end of the talk, what audience action or response qualifies as a win? In other words, what do I want my listeners to do as a result of hearing my presentation?)

In the last chapter, you learned about the importance of structure. All talks need to be organized in some manner. Remember that this organization can be as extensive as a word-for-word manuscript or as simple as a few key words. Always make sure that your message is organized in a way that amply addresses your subject and leads the audience toward your "desired outcome." Now, it is time to return to the beginning of the message and discuss the introduction.

The Introduction

The ninety-second rule is related to the introduction of your talk. In essence, you have about ninety seconds to hook your listeners or you will probably lose them. Sensory input in our society has multiplied exponentially over the past two decades, with the attention span of the average person now greatly diminished. Among youth, it is even more pronounced. In this day and age, speakers must grab the audience's attention quickly, and this is best done with the aid of an effective introduction. Think of the introduction as a window into your message.

For a minute, let's go back to the mall. Most of us know what it is to window shop. We stroll through the mall from store to store looking in the windows. Have you noticed that some window displays are better than others? Some businesses pay very careful attention to up-front displays while others seem to take a more haphazard approach. Smart businesses recognize the importance of their front windows. These visual showcases can enhance a business' image and advertise the store's contents to passersby. Many stores hire specially trained display experts hoping to lure customers into their store.

The introduction of your message is kind of like a showcase window that gives an audience a glimpse into your talk. If it is not enticing, or if it fails to grab the listeners' attention, they will immediately check out. If an audience checks out during your opening comments, it is quite difficult to get them back. Therefore, it is crucial that your introduction is carefully crafted and designed to hook the audience quickly.

Consider the following two introductions presented to a group of female seniors. Which of these introductions causes you to want to hear more? The talk was entitled, "Tips for Surviving a Holdup."

Introduction One

Good morning! My name is Bill and it is good to see so many of you interested in my presentation. I hope at the end of my talk you will feel it was a valuable use of your time. Today I'm here to talk with you about safety. Safety is important, especially as we get older. When it comes to safety, there are many things we could discuss. For instance, we could talk about auto safety, home safety, online safety, or a variety of other safety-related issues. However, today I'd like to address a subject few people think much about. Recently, I have met several senior citizens who were the victims of robbery. Some were robbed at knifepoint, others were held up at gunpoint. For this reason, I thought it might be helpful to advise you on some "Tips for Surviving a Holdup." Of course, my hope is that none of you will ever need to use these tips, but just in case, it would be wise to pay careful attention.

Introduction Two

My seventy-eight year old Aunt Alice loves to walk. A few years ago, she was taking a stroll through an outdoor mall on a warm summer afternoon. Suddenly, she saw him. In an instant, he was in her face grabbing at her purse. In those terrifying moments, my aunt recalls her heart pounding as her handbag was ripped from her shoulder. She watched in disbelief as her favorite purse and her social security check disappeared around a corner in the hands a cruel and callous thief.

"In a moment," she said to me, "I knew my life could have ended. I was so unprepared for something like this. I never thought it could happen to me!"

What would you have done if you were my Aunt Alice? Did you know that there are proven tips for surviving a holdup? These tips come directly from the police department. They gave them to me and I'm here today to give those tips to you. I'm going to ask you to memorize them. So please, take out a pencil and paper. It is time to start writing them down.

At the risk of pointing out the obvious, the second introduction is much more of an attention grabber. It heightens my desire to hear the rest of the talk. While the first introduction works, it lacks punch and is missing a powerful personal hook. On the other hand, the second introduction includes all the elements of a good introduction.

For those of you who were actually hooked by the second introduction, here are the tips for surviving a holdup according to the Arlington, Virginia Police Department:

What Should I Do If I am a Robbery Victim?

DO NOT PANIC—get a grip on yourself and stay calm. Take some deep breaths.

DO NOT RESIST—the robber wants your valuables, not you. "Things" can always be replaced ... you cannot.

OBEY THE ROBBER'S INSTRUCTIONS—listen closely to what the robber says and do not argue. Try to remember the exact words spoken by the robber as it may help with the police investigation.

BE ALERT—notice what is happening.

LOOK FOR DISTINGUISHING CHARACTERISTICS —look for things that cannot be changed, such as scars, marks, tattoos, limps, accents, etc.

WEAPONS—take careful note of any weapon. You will have to describe it later to the police. If the robber indicates that there is a weapon in his pocket, assume it is a gun. If the robber has a gun, assume it is loaded.

DESCRIPTION OF ROBBER—compare the robber to your own height and weight to estimate the size of your attacker.

COOPERATE WITH THE POLICE—if you are robbed, or see someone else being robbed, report it to the police immediately. [5]

5 Police Department, Arlington, Virginia
(www.arlingtonva.us/Departments/Police/citizens/reference/crime_prevention/
PoliceCitizensReferenceCrime_preventionRobbery.aspx

Introductions: Four Essentials

Now let's look at four essential elements found in effective introductions. *First, effective introductions capture the audience's attention.* In other words, listeners want to hear more. In the example above, the opening story about "Aunt Alice" grabs my attention right away.

Second, effective introductions surface a need in the listener. In the above illustration, a hearer wants and needs to pay close attention because, "Knowing these tips could save my life. I now realize that this could actually happen to me." That is what makes the introduction relevant.

Third, effective introductions clearly identify the subject, "Tips for surviving a holdup."

Fourth, effective introductions point to the desired outcome. In this case, the desired outcome is to get the audience to write down and memorize the "tips for surviving a hold-up."

The introduction is the first step in winning or losing your audience. Unlike baseball batters, when it comes to introductions, speakers do not get multiple swings. We only get one chance per talk to make contact, and we had better hit at least a single. By paying careful attention to the four essential elements above, you will ensure that your audience is engaged from the start. Who knows, if you work at it, you might even hit a home run.

Remember that the introduction must make people feel like they need and want to hear more. Just as the ground must be tilled before planting, so listeners must be readied for teaching. The four elements mentioned above will help prep the audience to want to hear more of what you have to say. Therefore, it will serve us well to examine each of these elements more closely.

ELEMENT ONE:
CAPTURE THE AUDIENCE'S ATTENTION

The first essential element of an effective introduction requires that we quickly capture the audience's attention. This can be achieved by opening with a gripping story, thought-provoking questions, a bold statement, surprising statistical facts, etc. Of course, there are many other ways to initiate a talk, but these are the most common approaches.

We All Love Stories: There is something magical about a well-told story that draws us in. Presenters and aspiring speakers should learn to become good storytellers. One way to do this is by practicing telling stories. Record yourself telling stories. Talk about an interesting personal experience. Take the time to retell a nursery rhyme or a Bible story. You can also make up stories. Use your imagination. Whenever possible, read stories and books about storytelling. By doing any or all these suggestions you will surely improve your own storytelling abilities.

Thought-provoking questions are also a great technique for hooking your audience. Recently, Tara a young server at Starbucks told me she was taking a college speech class. Her teacher asked her to do a demonstration talk for the class. He gave her the option to choose whatever she wanted to demonstrate. Most mornings she serves me coffee. She also knows that I work with public speakers. So she decided to solicit my help. She wanted suggestions for her five-minute demonstration talk. I thought for a moment and asked her if she had ever made guacamole, and she said yes she had.

"Do you find that it is messy to make?" I asked, and she quickly agreed. So I suggested that she demonstrate "How to Make Guacamole Without Making a Mess." She thought that might be fun, but did not know quite how to do it. I instructed her to put all the ingredients in a quart-size plastic bag and knead them together until mixed. Then simply cut one of the bottom corners off the bag and squeeze it out. Voila! Guacamole without the mess!

She thought that sounded like a fun idea, so she decided to try it. I am not sure how she introduced her talk, but she did get a "B" on it, for which she was very happy. Her teacher told her that he graded her down because she lost connection with her audience while she was making the guacamole.

How would you introduce this short demonstration talk? I might have introduced it this way:

Have you ever made a mess while making something in the kitchen? How many of you like cleaning up those kinds of messes? [Pause] I don't either! I have a confession to make. I love guacamole and so do most of my friends. They all think I make the best guacamole in the world. It's true, I do. Even so, I used to hate making it because it was so messy, that is until recently. A few weeks ago I learned how to make Guacamole without making a mess.

Next time you have a party, pick up some tortilla chips and make a batch of guacamole the way I am about to show you. It's easy and your friends will love it. I am excited to show you how to make guacamole without making a mess. Are you ready? Here's how you do it....

Asking and Answering Questions: In the previous example, we see how to use simple questions to draw the audience into your subject. Questions can be pointed, provocative, funny, or deadly serious. The subject matter helps determine what kinds of questions are best suited for a given introduction. Generally, it is a good idea to ask at least one question in your introduction because questions are great tools for quickly stimulating audience thinking and interest. However, always remember that if you ask questions, you must answer them sometime during your talk. Let me give you an example.

Suppose I am speaking to a group of young business owners. The title of my talk is, "How to Avoid Wasting Money on Advertising." The first few lines of the introduction could sound like this:

Most business owners spend significant amounts of money on advertising. But few really know if that money is well spent. Are you wasting your hard earned dollars on ineffective advertising? How can you measure the rate of return on the money you spend?

The questions above require answers. One of my speech professors taught me, "In your introduction never scare up more rabbits than you can shoot." In other words, do not ask questions or raise issues you are not prepared to address. If you do, you will leave your audience annoyed and perplexed.

In the business example above, at least two questions would need to be answered during the presentation. First, how can I determine if I am wasting money on advertising?

Second, how can I measure the rate of return on my advertising expenditures? To reiterate, questions are great tools to use in your introduction, but at some point they must be answered.

Bold Statements: Bold statements can also be helpful when introducing a subject. These statements arouse attention, particularly when used in the introduction. Here is an example of a bold statement: *"Today, I will show you how to increase your profits by twenty percent in only thirty days without spending a dime!"* Obviously, if you said this to the right crowd, it would garner a lot of interest. Nevertheless, you had better be able to back up your words with reality.

Statistics: Another tip for garnering the audience's attention in your introduction is using an informative or shocking statistic. For instance, "Eighty-five percent of all children who show behavior disorders come from fatherless homes – 20 times the average."[6] This alarming statistic is an attention grabber and could easily introduce a message on "The Impact of Divorce on Children."

The key to using statistics in any part of your presentation is to ensure that they are verifiably accurate. Many speakers learn this lesson the hard way. Highlighting vital statistics can heighten interest in your talk. However, using inaccurate statistics can spread misinformation. Do not hesitate to use statistics, but use them well. Whenever possible, cite the source of the information you are providing. This will place the credit where it belongs.

6 Center for Disease Control

ELEMENT TWO:
SURFACE A NEED IN THE LISTENER

The second element of an effective introduction involves surfacing a relevant need in the listener. The glue that helps your introduction stick to the listener is *relevance*. Failure to make your subject quickly relevant is one of the fastest ways to lose the audience's attention. Relevance answers questions about the message's value to the listener, questions such as, "Why should this message matter to me?" or, "Why should I care about what you are saying"? Presenters must never assume that listeners will arrive at these answers alone. They need to be told and told again why listening will benefit them.

If you hope to keep an audience's attention, you must demonstrate the message's relevance to them throughout the talk, not just in the introduction. Nevertheless, establishing relevance is especially important during the introduction. Speakers must instruct listeners "why" they should pay attention. In other words, how will they benefit from listening? Without raising a need and establishing a sense of value, we give the audience very little reason to listen.

Suppose you are doing a talk at the PTA (Parents Teachers Association). The message title is, "Why We Need Parents in the Classroom." What would a relevant introduction—one that surfaces a need —look like in this setting? Compare the following two introductions. Which of the two introductions raises the need and your interest more?

Introduction One:

Hi, I'm Betty . I have been a parent volunteer for a number of years. I was actually named parent volunteer of the year two years running. Obviously, I am very proud of that achievement. I have to admit, I am hoping to win it again this year. Even though I do not know you all, I do know that all of you are interested in your child's education. You have proven that in part by being here tonight. I know you agree that our kids' education is not only this school's duty and responsibility but yours and mine as well. Frankly, I have a hard time understanding why more parents do not volunteer and get involved. Why is it so difficult for us to find parents to help out in our classrooms? I'm here tonight to tell you that we could really use your help. We are way down on the number of classroom volunteers this year, and it is putting added pressure on our teachers. I'd like you to consider signing up as a volunteer. The need is immediate and again, we really need your help. Tonight, I want to take a few minutes and familiarize you with what our parent volunteers do in the classroom. After this talk, I will be in the back of the room with a signup sheet for those of you interested in helping us. Now let me tell you what you will be doing if you choose to volunteer . . .

Introduction Two

Good evening! Thanks for being here tonight. The other morning I saw one of our kindergarten teachers standing outside of her classroom. She was crying. It concerned me, so I approached her and asked, "What is wrong"? I was interested not just because my daughter Laney is

94

in her kindergarten class, but because she is such a great teacher. After wiping the tears away, she told me that she was feeling a bit overwhelmed. This year her class size increased to forty children and she lost her parent volunteer. After a couple of minutes, she thanked me for my concern and went back into her classroom to attend to her students. I walked away feeling concerned and quite ashamed. Here is why. I remember getting two letters from the school asking for help. I ignored them both. However, putting a face on the need has made all the difference for me. Yesterday, after dropping Laney off at class, I went straight to the office and signed up to be a parent volunteer. This morning was my first day in the classroom. I want to tell you what it was like. But, before I do, I want you to know that we need more help, to be exact, seven more volunteers. When was the last time you visited your child's classroom? I regret that it took me so long. You should have seen the smile on that teacher's face when I walked into the classroom this morning. She told me that I made her day. I am passing out signup cards right now. I'm hoping at least seven of you will join me. Now, let me tell you about my first day in the classroom . . .

Well, what do you think? Which of the two introductions made the subject most real for you? My guess is that you are saying introduction two. The first introduction is adequate, although it is a bit self-indulgent and sterile. The second introduction is more compelling because it makes the issue real to me as a parent.

Introductions that fail to make the subject relevant or surface a need will inevitably fall flat, so make sure you continually emphasize and reinforce why what you are saying should matter to the listening audience. You cannot assume they will connect the dots on their own.

Tell Them Why It Matters: One way to highlight relevance, and to surface a need, is by inserting occasional comments and questions that draw attention to the message's value. Presenters are wise to say things such as, "Here is why this matters." Or, "Let me tell you why this should be of interest to you." Questions like these also draw attention to the relevance: "Do you see how this impacts you?" Or, "Do you know why I'm telling you this?"

In summary, in your introduction and throughout your message, continue stressing why what you are saying is important to the audience. (In the next chapter, you will learn how illustrations can assist you in this regard.)

ELEMENT THREE:
IDENTIFY THE SUBJECT

The third element of an effective introduction is that it identifies the subject of the talk. This may seem obvious, but many speakers fall short here. Surprisingly, many introductions do not succeed in helping listeners identify the subject. This forces the audience to hunt for the topic in a sea of many words. Unfortunately, some speakers make distinguishing the subject even more complicated. These presenters go on to complete the introduction but neglect mentioning the subject. Sadly, this robs the introduction of part of its intended use and creates confusion in the minds of the audience.

Effective introductions accentuate the subject so that it is crystal clear. From the outset, the audience should know what the speaker is talking about. At the end of a good introduction listeners ought to be able to state the subject in a plain sentence.

There is a simple way to test your introductions to discover if your subject is readily identifiable. This test will ensure that your topic is clear to potential hearers. Prior to giving a talk, share your introduction with a colleague or friend. It will only take a couple of minutes. When you are finished, ask them to tell you in a sentence the subject of your talk. If they cannot do it, or worse give you a wrong answer, then, "Houston, we have a problem!" Obviously, if those you test cannot identify your subject, the same will be true for the real audience. Go back and work on it until your subject is easily identifiable.

Now let's look at two more introductions and see which one you think makes the subject crystal clear:

Introduction One:

Internet shopping makes buying easy. A few weeks ago, I bought a new watch online. I bought it in about ten minutes. It would have taken me at least two hours to get to the mall and purchase that same watch. However, as easy as it was to buy, there was a huge problem. The watch I purchased was a fake. I thought I was buying a Rolex, but instead, I discovered I purchased a knock-off watch with the Rolex name on it. Since then I have been hesitant to shop online. That is, until the other day.

Earlier this week a friend introduced me to a website that talks a lot about shopping online. It helped me see where I went wrong. Today, I have come to talk about my experience in the hope that you will not get burned like I did. So for the next few minutes we are going to talk about shopping online. I will also tell you where I ended up finding a good deal on a real Rolex . . .

Introduction Two:

Online shopping makes shopping easy, but you have to be careful. Have you ever lost money shopping online? [Pause] I have! Last week I lost $1,200, when I bought a fake Rolex watch over the Internet. Is online shopping safe? Most of time, yes, but you have to follow certain guidelines. After the fake Rolex incident, a friend introduced me to a website that specializes in teaching people guidelines for safe online shopping. This website lists a number of guiding principles to help protect you from scams when you are shopping over the Internet. Today I am going to share those guidelines with you so that you do not lose money like I did. These guidelines are designed to protect you from Internet thieves. Please write them down and use them the next time you shop online. By the way, I used these guidelines and bought a real Rolex at a great price. Are you ready to write? Here are the guidelines . . .

The first introduction does a poor job of defining the talk's subject. It would be easy to come up with a few different possibilities. On the other hand, introduction two makes the subject quite obvious, "Guidelines for Safe Online Shopping." An effective introduction must never leave the audience confused or guessing about the subject.

ELEMENT FOUR:
POINT TO THE "DESIRED OUTCOME"

The fourth essential element of an effective introduction involves pointing the audience to the desired outcome. The introduction needs to nudge the audience toward your predetermined objective. The introduction is meant to unfold the first step in this journey. It shows the audience a glimpse into your desired outcome. Allow me to illustrate.

Recently, I spoke to a group of college students about "How to Prepare a Ten-Minute Talk on Any Subject." Knowing from the outset where I wanted to end up helped shape my opening remarks. Frankly, I don't remember the exact introduction, but I do recall it sounding something like this:

How to Prepare a Ten-Minute Talk on Any Subject

Introduction:

What if someone asked you to speak in front of this class for ten minutes? And they told you that you could choose any subject you like? How would you prepare that talk? What would you do first? What would you do next? Well, I have a surprise for you. Someone is asking you to prepare a ten-minute talk on a subject of your choice. I am that someone! And the talks I'm referring to will begin next week. [Pause] By that gasp and the look on your faces, I know you are worried. Please don't be. I am here to help you learn how to prepare and deliver the assigned talks. Today, I will be teaching you,

*"How to prepare a ten-minute talk on any subject." I
suggest you pay careful attention for the next few minutes. Listen closely and you will learn how to prepare
and deliver a ten-minute talk on any subject. It might
surprise you, but our preparation does not focus first on
you! Instead, it begins with asking, "What do I know
about my audience? Are you ready? Let's get started . . .*

College students have a lot on their plates. My introduction had to break through a lot of distractions and clut-
ter. It also needed to get their attention, highlight the subject,
and surface a need to listen. Finally, it had to begin pointing them toward my desired outcome—in this case, getting
ready to prepare and deliver a ten-minute talk.

The opening remarks of your presentations should address and include all four elements mentioned above. Let's
review those four essential elements once again. First, effective introductions capture the audience's attention. Second,
they surface a need and give the audience a reason "why"
they should listen. Third, they identify the subject. Fourth,
they point listeners to the desired outcome. Paying careful
attention to these four essential elements is sure to improve
your introductions and thus your presentations.

The introduction is a bit like the first few notes of a
song. If the opening is out of tune, my assumption is that the
rest of the song will be as well. Conversely, if those first few
notes are audibly appealing and finely tuned, they will draw
me in and make me want to hear the rest of the song. When
you speak, make sure your introduction sings and that it is
in tune with the rest of your message. If you do, it won't be
long before your audience is humming along with you.

More on Transitions

It is almost time to move beyond the introduction and into the core of the message. However, before doing that, it is useful to talk a little more about transitions. The closing words of your opening remarks should serve as a bridge statement or transition. This transition connects the introduction with the main body of your presentation. Bridge or transition statements are relatively simple to create. They usually consist of one or two sentences that serve to link one component of your structure to another. For instance, a transition might connect your "introduction" to your "first movement." Here is an example of a transition statement connecting an introduction to the initial movement or point:

Tools for Resolving Conflict in the Workplace

Transition statement at the end of the introduction:

Resolving conflict between co-workers is not easy. It always takes time and generally requires the use of proven techniques. Today, we will examine three proven practices for resolving conflict, specifically, conflict in the workplace. The first practice is "The Importance of Listening"...

Notice the introduction ends with a transition statement designed to serve as a bridge to the first movement or point. In this case, the first movement is "The Importance of Listening."

Think of transition statements as "links" joining one element of your talk to the next. Have you ever seen a string of sausage? As a child, we used to visit an Italian deli that made the best sausage. They sold it by the string, and you could get as many or as few as you liked. The sausages were linked together by a small bit of twisted casing. That little twist connected one sausage to the next. Transition statements are like those small connectors. They link one element of your talk seamlessly to the next. Without carefully thought-out transition statements, the elements of a presentation can lose their distinctiveness and bleed into one another. However, using well-crafted transition statements sets up each element and helps move listeners from one component to another with more fluidity. Whenever you find a choppy connection between elements, use a transition statement. It will help your presentation sound much more cohesive.

CHAPTER 7

Pointed vs. Pointless Illustrations

"A WISELY CHOSEN ILLUSTRATION IS
ALMOST ESSENTIAL TO FASTEN THE TRUTH
UPON THE ORDINARY MIND, AND NO
TEACHER CAN AFFORD TO NEGLECT THIS
PART OF HIS PREPARATION."

–Howard Crosby

In a talk, illustrations are word pictures that clarify, support, exemplify, or demonstrate points in the message. Basically, there are two kinds of illustrations: "pointed" and "pointless." A pointed illustration supports the subject while a pointless one does not. Pointed illustrations further clarify the subject and lend a hand in moving listeners ever closer to a predetermined desired outcome. Pointless illustrations may be interesting to hear, but they fail in their intended mission. Ultimately, they do not support the subject or put emphasis on the predetermined desired outcome.

> **Example of a Pointless Illustration:**
> *Recently, while listening to a presentation, I heard a pointless illustration. It was a great story, but totally unrelated to the subject of the talk. The title of the talk was "New Ways to Market Music." The subject peaked my interest because my granddaughter,*

> *Ashley, is an exceptionally talented singer, musician, and songwriter. I have happily committed to helping her advance her musical career. We had just completed her debut CD, so I was hoping to learn something from this seminar that would help me in marketing it. Unfortunately, the speaker spent very little time talking about music marketing. Instead, the majority of his talk was dedicated to self-promotion and random industry stories unrelated to the advertised topic. Frankly, it was a colossal waste of time.*

Pointed illustrations support and clarify some key aspect of the message and nudge the audience a step closer to the presenter's intended goal. Years ago, I spoke to a group of career-aged singles about "Building Blocks of Good Character." My first movement in the talk was "A Commitment to Honesty."

Everyone has heard the expression, "Honesty is the best policy." Nevertheless, it is easier said than done. The temptation to lie is ever before us, and, quite often, it looks like the "best" option. I recall using the following pointed illustration during the first movement of that talk. What you are about to read is a true story. It happened to me.

Title: " Building Blocks of Good Character"
Movement One: "A Commitment to Honesty"
Illustration:

When was the last time you were tempted to lie? Recently, I was driving down the road listening to the radio. A great old Bon Jovi song came on, and I decided to sing along. Just as I was about to belt out the chorus, I saw the policeman. He was sitting on a motorcycle holding a radar gun that was pointed at me. I had passed a sign a way back that said 25 MPH. I immediately looked down and saw I was going 38 miles per hour. Whoops! In a moment, the red light was flashing, and I pulled over. I thought to myself, I have got to lie. I cannot just admit that I was speeding. Maybe I can convince him that his radar gun is defective. Alternatively, tell him I was just going a little bit over the speed limit. Suddenly, he was standing outside the car motioning for me to roll down my window. A hundred lies were on the tip of my tongue. The next thing I knew, he was asking me the proverbial question, "Did you know how fast you were going?" What I said next surprised us both. "I know exactly how fast I was going. When I saw you, I looked down, and the speedometer read 38MPH." Immediately, I closed my eyes, lowered my head anticipating a tongue-lashing and a fat ticket. Shocked by my admission, he asked, "What did you say?" I repeated my confession and this time looked up at his face. To my amazement, he was smiling. Then he said, "You are the first person that hasn't lied to me all day." I am going to reward your honesty by not giving you the ticket you deserve. But, you have to promise me two things: First, you will not speed through here again, and second, that you will take an old person to lunch." I could not believe my ears. I thanked him profusely, gave him my word on both counts, drove to the nearest McDonalds and, fulfilling one promise, I took myself out to lunch. (I'm just kidding!) The following week, I really did take

105

an old person out to lunch. Regrettably, honesty does not always pay off like this. Most often, even when you are honest, you still get the ticket, but you drive away with a clear conscience, and that night you may get a better night's sleep.

Here is why this is a positive example of a pointed illustration. First, it supports the subject by highlighting one of the building blocks of good character, namely, "A Commitment to Honesty." Second, it prepares students to write down the benefits of good character, which is ultimately my desired outcome. In this case, the building block is "a commitment to honesty," and the benefit is "a clear conscience" resulting in a peaceful night's sleep.

Use Canned Illustrations Cautiously

There are literally thousands of illustrations available online, some for sale, others free. Occasionally, "canned" illustrations are useful. However, be careful not to use them too often. The reason is that they tend to get dated and overused. Here is an example of a canned illustration found on the Internet. Unfortunately, no author was cited.

Subject: Overcoming Life's Challenges
Illustration:

One day a donkey fell into an old well. From a distance, the rancher heard the donkey crying out in hope of being rescued. Hearing the donkey in distress the rancher ran to the well. After examining the situation he concluded

106

that the donkey was too old to survive a rescue attempt. Lacking an alternative solution, the rancher decided to fill the old well with dirt and bury the donkey. He reasoned that this would end the donkey's suffering. The rancher enlisted the help of a neighbor, and they began shoveling dirt into the hole and onto the donkey. Immediately, the donkey realized what was happening. He cried out even louder, yet the determined rancher and his neighbor just kept shoveling. For the next few minutes he continued to make awful noises but soon, to their relief, the noise stopped and everything grew quiet. After a while, the farmer looked down into the well. He was absolutely astonished by what he saw. The donkey was still alive, and progressing towards the top of the well. He discovered that by shaking off the dirt instead of letting it cover him, he could keep stepping on top of it and the floor level would rise. Soon the donkey could step up over the edge of the well, and happily, trotted off. From time to time, life shovels dirt on top of each of us. The trick is to shake it off and use it to take a step up.

Canned illustrations can stimulate our thinking. They can also serve as fodder for creating new illustrations or updating old ones. This is a great way to use them. But be careful not to rely too much on common illustrations because it is unnecessary. Everyday life is filled with countless illustrations. Be diligent to jot them down. Make a habit of recording noteworthy incidents, lessons, examples, and stories. Clip articles and interesting tidbits from newspapers, magazines, and periodicals. Start building an illustration file indexed by subject. Add to it often. This file will serve you well over the years. You will soon discover that all speakers experience dry periods when it comes to creativity. During those creative gaps, you will have a source of quality illustrations in the bank.

Pointed illustrations are so important. They can change a black-and-white talk into one that is alive with color. They clarify, unpack, explain, and illuminate points in vivid and memorable ways. Pointed illustrations also aid speakers in ushering listeners toward their desired outcome.

In most presentations, key movements or points need supporting illustrations. Obviously, there are exceptions. Even though pointed illustrations are crucial to a good presentation, here, a cautionary note is in order because it is possible to over illustrate a talk. Illustrations must be used sparingly to support *key* points, not *every* point. If they are overused, they can take from, rather than add to, a given message. Too many illustrations can confound and confuse the audience. Overusing illustrations also dilutes the impact of those you've used correctly.

Most everyone has heard of a surge protector. It is used to protect electrical devices from too much power. The computer I am using right now requires a certain amount of electricity to function properly. If it gets too much power, it will be ruined. The same is true when it comes to messages. The right amount of illustrations can significantly enhance a talk while too many will ruin it. When used properly, illustrations will spice up an otherwise vanilla presentation. There is an old and familiar expression, "a picture is worth a thousand words." So rather than talking further about illustrations, I'd prefer to show you some.

Examples of Pointed Illustrations

Below are three different pointed illustrations. First, we will look at one from John Maxwell that supports "team building." Then, there is an illustration from Barbara Glanz that accentuates "customer service." Finally, we will look at an illustration from Wayne Cordeiro that focuses on "values." These illustrations exemplify high quality, illuminate the subject, and move listeners toward each presenter's desired outcome.

THE LAW OF MT. EVEREST

"When A Challenge Escalates Teamwork Must Elevate"

For those unfamiliar with John Maxwell, he is a leadership expert, speaker, and author who has sold over 13 million books. His organizations have trained two million leaders worldwide.

The people on your team have the potential to grow. I say to leaders, if the people on your team are the same as they were last year, you have not done your job. I say to team members, if you are the same as you were last year, you have not done your job. The law of Mt. Everest says, "The bigger the challenge the better the team needs to develop." Do not go after the big dream first; develop the team, and then go after the dream.

This is a true story about a guide who took a team up Mt. Everest. They got about two-thirds of the way up, ran into a major storm, and had to come back down. Because of extensive preparation and significant travel expenses, everyone was very disappointed. The guide, knowing the disappointment of the team, said before they left for home that they would have dinner together. Obviously, at the dinner there was a somber mood. For that reason, it was kind of a low-key night. After the meal, the guide stood up before the group and said, "I want to share something with you." Behind him on the wall was a huge picture of Mt. Everest. It was as big as the wall. The guide turned his back on the group and began talking to the picture. He said, "Mt. Everest, we tried to climb to the top. We tried to conquer you, but we failed. We had to come back down. I want you to know that today you defeated us. But Mt. Everest, I want to say something else. We are coming back again next year. And Mt. Everest, I want you to know when we come back next year we will defeat you. Let me tell you why. Mt. Everest you are as big as you are ever going to be." Then the guide turned from the picture to the group and said, "But the people on this team, they can get bigger." That is the law of Mt. Everest. Gather and grow your team. Then take on that dream and go all the way to the top.

BUILDING CUSTOMER LOYALTY
"One Person Can Make a Difference"

Barbara Glanz heads up her own communication company. She is a seasoned corporate and organizational trainer who has spoken on seven continents and all fifty states. Below is a paraphrased version of one of her illustrations.

A few years ago I was asked to speak to three thousand employees of a large grocery chain. After I had spoken, as is my tradition, I gave out my home phone number to the audience. Not too long after, I had a young man call my home. He told me his name was Johnny, and that he was a bagger in one of the grocery stores. He also told me that he was a person with Down syndrome. During the call Johnny said, "Barbara, I liked what you said. So I went home that night and asked my dad to help me with the computer. We set up the computer to do three columns. Every night from that night forward I would go home and find a thought for the day. If I could not find one that I liked, I would think one up. Then dad and I typed out the thought six times on a page, printed out fifty pages, cut them out, and I signed my name on the back." He told me that the next day, he put a thought for the day in every person's groceries he bagged.

Now about a month later the store manager of John-ny's store called me and said, Barbara, I want to tell you what happened earlier today. When I went out on the floor about 9:30 this morning, the line at Johnny's checkout was three times longer than any other line. I went ballistic, I was yelling, "Get more people out here, get more lines open!" However, the customers said, "No, no, we want to be in Johnny's lane. We want the thought for the day!"

Now I ask you, who do you think is the most impor-tant person in that whole store? One woman told the manager, "I only used to shop here once a week, but now I come in every time I drive by because I want the thought for the day."

Three months later the store manager called me back again and said, "Barbara, you and Johnny have trans-formed our store." He went on to say, "Before in the

111

floral department, when we had a broken off flower or unused corsages, we would just throw them away. Now, our employees go out onto the floor and find an elderly woman or a little girl and pin it on them. One of our meat packers loves Snoopy, so we ordered fifty thousand Snoopy stickers. Now every time he packages a piece of meat, he puts a Snoopy sticker on it." I said to him, "Well, I don't know about dog stickers on the meat!" [Laughter] The manager concluded by saying, "We are having so much fun and our customers are having so much fun." Now that is the story of a true leader. If Johnny can do it, there is no reason that every one of us in this room cannot do the same. When it comes to customer service, one person can make a difference.

TRANSITIONING A CHURCH CULTURE
"How Values Influence Culture"

Several years ago I attended a seminar put on by a church. The keynote speaker was a pastor named Wayne Cordeiro. He is the founding pastor of New Hope Christian Fellowship (enewhope.org) on the island of Oahu in Hawaii. About 14,000 people attend his church on a weekly basis. Since then, he has become both a trusted mentor and a very dear friend. His reputation as a world-class speaker is well known both in and outside Christian circles. On this particular day, the subject of his talk was "Transitioning a Church Culture." Often, I consult businesses and nonprofit organizations on issues related to culture. Because of this, the subject was of particular interest to me. During his talk, Pastor Cordeiro talked about the role of values in shaping the culture of a church. This is true in business and organizations as well. He asked those attending a poignant question: "What values do you want your children to live out twenty years from now? The values they live out in the future are directly related to

112

*those that characterize the culture they live in today." He then
reinforced that statement with a pointed illustration. Here is a
paraphrase of it:*

*The story goes that prior to starting a new village, Inuit
elders meet together. Their intent is to determine the
kind of men and women that they want their children to
grow up to be as adults. Around the fire one elder says,
"This is a hard land, we need our children to be strong."
The chief elder asks of the group, "What animal represents strength?" One the elders replies, "The bear is
strong." And so they take a long wooden pole, and they
carve the face of a bear on the bottom of it.*

*The chief asks again, "What other qualities do we
want our children to embrace as they grow up? Another
replies, "This is a difficult land. Our children must learn
to persevere." The chief said, "Someone name a creature
that represents perseverance." An elder responds, "The
Salmon perseveres." "Good," says the chief, "Let us
carve the image of a salmon on the pole above the bear."*

*Another elder says, "This is a dangerous land and
our children must stay vigilant." "Well said," replied
the chief, "Carve the head of an owl above that of the
salmon."*

*For those of you unfamiliar with this kind of pole,
it is called a "totem pole". Totem poles are placed in
the center of a settlement to display the village's values. When the young boy approaches his father and
asks, "Dad, why is that bear on the pole?" his father
replies, "Son, I am so glad you asked. As you grow up,
you will learn this is a hard land and the bear represents strength to remind you to be strong." When the*

113

young girl asks her mother about the salmon, she is told about perseverance. And so on. Now it is time to ask you, as church leaders, a question. If your church had a totem pole, what values would be carved there? In other words, what values characterize your community of faith? Whether you know it or not, those values are shaping your children's lives and future. For that reason, I strongly encourage you to revisit and, if necessary, revise those values. Our children are dependent upon us getting it right!

I hope the three examples above help you understand how a good "pointed illustration" can help you illuminate, demonstrate, and clarify some aspect of your subject and nudge your listeners ever closer to your predetermined outcome.

A Picture is Worth a Thousand Words

Mrs. Martin showed up for a hastily called parent/teacher conference with her third grade daughter's teacher. During the meeting, she learned that Katie was stirring up trouble among her classmates. Despite warnings, Katie continued to gossip and spread rumors about other students, and her incessant gossip was fueling deep divisions between several of her classmates. After a private chat with Katie's mom, the little girl was called into the office.

Her teacher, with the full backing of her mother, reiterated the importance of Katie putting an end to her troublesome habit. She explained to her that several children were profoundly hurt by her careless words. At the end of the meeting, Katie was asked to join the teacher and her mother out on the playground. As they exited the building, Katie was surprised to see her teacher carrying a pillow and a pair of scissors. When they got outside the wind was blowing briskly. Katie watched in amazement as her teacher cut off one end of the feather pillow. She then walked toward Katie and, suddenly, began shaking the pillow violently. The wind blew the feathers everywhere. Katie could not help but laugh. However, her laughter was short lived. Immediately, her teacher put down the featherless pillowcase walked closer to Katie and knelt down in front of her. She then looked at her and said, "Now, go and pick up every feather."

Katie looked at her teacher and her mom and knew they were not kidding. Although the request seemed silly, Katie began picking up the feathers. Unfortunately, every time she gathered a handful of feathers a strong wind came and blew them away. After a few minutes, Katie quit. She slowly and sadly walked back to where her teacher and mom were standing and with tears welling up in her eyes said, "I can never pick up every feather, even if I had a hundred years." Her teacher got back down on one knee and with a kind expression on her face and said, "Katie, I know you cannot pick up all the feathers. Neither will you ever be able to recover any of the careless and unkind words that you say about others."

With that, Katie closed her eyes and bowed her head. The teacher could see that Katie got the message. On that day, a little girl discovered the truth about gossip. She learned this valuable lesson from a teacher who knew this old Hassidic tale and that "a picture is worth a thousand words!"

CHAPTER 8

Finishing Strong

"I HEAR AND I FORGET, I SEE AND I
REMEMBER. I DO AND I UNDERSTAND."
– Chinese Proverb

Several years ago I registered to run a marathon in Kansas City. God only knows what I was thinking. For those unfamiliar with the distance of a marathon, it is exactly twenty-six miles, three-hundred-eighty-five yards. I made the decision to register about four months before the race. Prior to this, I had never been a long-distance runner. Sure, I had run as much as the next person, but never in a race as long as a marathon. At the time, none of my friends ran marathons, so I trained alone. Instead of being wise and reading up on the subject or speaking with other seasoned marathoners, I decided to figure the whole thing out on my own. This was not a wise decision.

My self-imposed training program consisted of running four to five days a week. By the time the marathon arrived, I was able to run up to twelve miles. My theory was that, on "game day," my adrenalin would carry me the rest of the way. Well, it made sense to me at the time.

The Kansas City Marathon is relatively flat, so I was confident I could tough it out. *I was so wrong.* On the day of the marathon, I actually ran just over eighteen miles before I hit "the wall." From that point forward, I walked and ran intermittently in order to complete the race. By the time I crossed the finish line, five hours and four minutes had elapsed, not exactly an Olympic pace. Although I did cross the finish line, I knew I had not finished strong. To this day, whenever I think of that marathon I do not focus on my valiant effort or the eighteen miles I ran so well. No, whenever I think of that marathon, I think of how poorly I finished.

A poor finish can ruin a good race, and the same is true when it comes to presentations. A poor conclusion can spoil an otherwise good talk. On the other hand, a well-crafted conclusion solidifies a presentation and leads to a powerful and purposeful finish.

The conclusion is the final part of your talk. Even though it is last, it is by no means least in importance. In fact, the contrary may be true because the conclusion is the culmination of all that has gone before it. You might say it is the climax of your presentation.

A well-crafted conclusion contains three components: (1) a concise review; (2) a specific request; and (3) a tangible reward. When joined together, these three components not only create a powerful conclusion, but also increase the likelihood that the speaker's desired outcome will be realized.

Now let's consider the significance and benefit of each component.

A Concise Review

The first component of a well-crafted conclusion is a concise review that reiterates and reinforces the movements or key points of the talk. This is a vital part of any meaningful

118

conclusion because it helps listeners retain key features of the presentation. Speakers often overestimate the audience's ability to hear and retain verbal communication. In today's information age, people are bombarded by so much sensory input that they are understandably guarded about what they choose to take in. Nowadays, people must actively filter the input coming at them. Many of us like digital recorders not only because they record our favorite TV shows, but also because they allow us to speed through unwanted commercials. This helps us minimize unwelcome data.

Reiterating the primary points in a message helps to highlight their value and importance. In addition, the repetition increases the likelihood that listeners will retain key portions of the message.

The Power of Repetition

Repetition is a powerful technique when it comes to retention. I have not seen a written copy of the Pledge of Allegiance since grade school, yet I can still recite it after more than fifty years. Do you know why? It's because of the *power of repetition*. When I was a young boy, we recited the Pledge of Allegiance every morning before class. Remembering the words of this Pledge so many years later proves the power of repetition. Hearing the Pledge of Allegiance over and over literally baked it into my memory.

Given this, it's no wonder why repetition is such a powerful and effective technique when incorporated into presentations, particularly conclusions. When used prudently, repetition greatly enhances recall and the audience's ability to memorize the talk's key points.

A Specific Request

The second component of a well-crafted conclusion is "a specific request." In other words, "What am I asking the audience to do?" Obviously, this request must dovetail with your predetermined desired outcome. You cannot assume the audience will figure out what you are asking them to do; you must be clear and specific.

Here is an example of a specific request: "Jot down two precise actions that will help you become a better team player. Commit to sharing those actions with your team within a week." Notice that the request is clear and specific, leaving no doubt about what you are asking them to do.

Avoid Assumption

One day a young boy named Billy was sitting in the kitchen chatting with his mom. After his daily school report, the conversation turned to the evening meal. Because Billy had been doing great at school and was also keeping up with his daily duties, his mom decided to let him pick whatever he wanted for dinner. Billy loved bacon, lettuce, and tomato sandwiches, especially when accompanied by a nice hot bowl of tomato soup and a side of potato chips. His mom knew she did not have what she needed in the cupboard, so she sent him on his first solo-shopping trip down the street to the corner store. Excited about the opportunity to do a "grownup thing," Billy left the house with twenty dollars and a big smile on his face. Soon he returned with a small bag of groceries and the appropriate change. When mom looked in the bag, she saw a can of tomato soup, a loaf of bread, two large tomatoes, a head of lettuce, and a bag of chips. Seeing that there was nothing else, she called him back into the kitchen and asked, "Where's the bacon?"

"You never told me to buy bacon," Billy said.

Mom shook her head and smiled. "You're right, I assumed you knew we needed it."

The moral of this story is simple. Unless you want your listeners to forget the bacon, you'd better be very clear and specific about what you're asking them to do.

A Tangible Reward

The third component of a well-crafted conclusion is offering a tangible reward, something that will help create an incentive so the audience will want to do what is being suggested. Keep in mind that listeners are always going to be thinking, "What's in it for me?" or "How will doing what I'm being asked to do benefit me?"

When audience members understand the benefit(s) of doing what the speaker is asking, they will be much more inclined to respond positively. One way to think of a tangible reward is in terms of cause and effect: "If you are willing to do this, you will get this." (This is also known as a conditional transaction.)

The offer of a reward is a great motivator, and people will often go to silly extremes if there is sufficient incentive. For instance, take NBC's TV show, "Minute to Win It." For those unfamiliar with the show, here's how it works. There are 10 challenges, each with a time limit of 60 seconds. If contestants finish all 10 challenges, they win $1 million. At select times during the show, contestants may choose to walk away with the money they have already won.

On this show, contestants do some of the goofiest things. One game is called "Bucket Head," the object of which is to bounce ping-pong balls off the floor and then off a wall and back into a bucket strapped atop the contestant's head. Another game called "Face the Cookie" requires contestants to move three Oreo cookies, one at a time, from their forehead to their mouth using only their faces. Now why would anyone do such foolish things in front of a nationwide TV audience? The answer is simple: *for a reward.* In this case, the incentive is potentially a lot of cash.

Practically speaking, most of us will not be offering cash prizes to listeners that do what we ask. If we want them to respond to our request, however, we had better offer something of value to them. Without an incentive, most listeners will default to inaction, so speakers need to help them recognize the personal benefit associated with acting on their specific request.

For example, suppose our subject is: "How to Get Promoted Faster." In the conclusion, it would be valuable to demonstrate the connection between getting a promotion and what you are asking listeners to do. It would also be helpful to reiterate the benefits (tangible reward) of getting a promotion (which should have been highlighted earlier in the talk). In this case, the listener must understand that a promotion will help them in tangible ways. For instance, a promotion would potentially give them greater influence in the organization, the opportunity to manage others, an increase in pay, and better overall benefits. These incentives increase the likelihood that the speaker's suggestions will be acted upon. In summary, one of the speaker's most important jobs is to help listeners answer their what's-in-it-for-me questions.

> *Remember, a well-crafted conclusion incorporates three components: a concise review, a specific request, and a tangible reward. These components must parallel and support the speaker's predetermined desired outcome. Your concluding remarks should remind listeners of the key points you have already told them (a concise review), call them to some kind of action (a specific request), and highlight the benefits of acting on that request (a tangible reward).*

A Sample Full-Length Conclusion to a Twenty-Minute Talk

I prefer not telling you the subject of this particular presentation until you finish reading the conclusion. My hope is that you will easily discover it on your own. I dedicate this to my former friend and colleague, Dan Tapson, who died February 17, 2010.

> *Now more than ever, you know why smoking is a dangerous and deadly habit. When a person smokes, they flirt with five harmful health risks. Let me reiterate those five risks one more time. The first is heart disease, second is stroke, the third is lung cancer, fourth is*

chronic bronchitis and emphysema, and the fifth is oral cancer. If you smoke, please quit. This decision can literally add years to your life. To help you quit, I am providing a list of resources. These organizations will support you as you battle this deadly addiction. If you do not smoke, please don't start. I have already proven statistically that smoking can and will shorten your life.

There may not be a fountain of youth, but there is a fast track to the grave, and it's smoking! Recently, I spoke at the memorial service of a dear friend, Dan Tapson. So many people loved Dan, including me. At his "celebration of life" ceremony, over three hundred people showed up to pay their last respects to this unique man. Unfortunately, for a short period of time, Dan had a smoking habit. He did not smoke his entire adult life. The tobacco did not need that long to infect his body.

In the last year of his life, Dan endured scores of doctor visits and treatments in a desperate attempt to stop the cancer from spreading to the rest of his body. On February 17, 2010, he died of lung cancer related to his smoking. I have already given you five good reasons to quit smoking. Now allow me to close with one more. When you smoke you endanger not only your own life but also the lives of those around you. When you quit smoking, you are not only reducing the risk to yourself, you are protecting those closest to you from the dangers of second-hand smoke. If you smoke, I plead with you to stop! Quit today! It just may save your life, and the life of someone you love.

For more information to help you quit smoking contact:
• *The National Cancer Institute: www.cancer.gov/ cancertopics/smoking*
• *California Smokers' Helpline: www.nobutts.ucsd.edu*
• *QuitNet: www.quitnet.com*

The title of the above talk was "Five Reasons to Quit Smoking." Notice that the conclusion included the three elements discussed earlier: a concise review, a specific request, and a tangible reward. In this case, the tangible reward was hope of a longer life for listeners and their loved ones.

CHAPTER 9

A Model "Purpose-Centered Talk"

"LONG IS THE ROAD TO LEARNING
BY PRECEPTS, BUT SHORT AND
SUCCESSFUL BY EXAMPLES."
– Proverb

Before seeing an example of a model purpose-centered talk, it is important to review the foregoing material. The following recap of things you've learned to this point will serve as both a review and somewhat of a template for the talk that follows.

Step 1: The speaker begins by answering four vital questions:

1. To whom am I speaking?
2. How much time do I have to speak?
3. What subject will I be addressing?
4. What is my desired outcome?

Step 2: Refine the subject to make sure it is a "single subject."

- The subject should be of interest and value to your listeners.
- The subject should be within your knowledge base. (If it is not, extensive research will be a must.)

127

- The subject should evoke a sense of passion in you.
- The subject must be age- and audience-appropriate.

Step 3: Once, you have a single subject, "begin at the end" and determine your desired outcome. What will you be asking the audience to do at the end of your talk?

Step 4: What type of talk will you be doing?

Type of Speech	*Goal*
Motivational	Call to Action
Demonstration	Show how to
Informational	Increase knowledge
Inspirational	Encourage
Opinion	Convince
Rebuttal	Repudiate
Acceptance	Acknowledge
Tribute	Celebrate
Sermon	Transform

Step 5: Choose your preferred structure (manuscript, full outline, movements, key words, etc.).

Step 6: What teaching method will you use: inductive, deductive, or another approach?

- The "Deductive" method looks like this: Principle Stated → Examples Given → Proof in Practice
- The "Inductive" method looks like this: Examples Given → Proof in Practice → Principle Stated

Step 7: Craft your introduction. Remember the "ninety-second rule" and the four essential elements found in powerful and purposeful introductions:

1. The introduction must capture the audience's attention.
2. The introduction must be relevant and surface a need.
3. The introduction must identify the subject.
4. The introduction must point the audience toward the predetermined desired outcome.

Step 8: Decide which "pointed illustrations" you will use to support your key points. Remember, pointed illustrations clarify, illuminate and/or demonstrate the subject and help nudge listeners toward your desired outcome.

Step 9: Formulate your conclusion. Recall that a well-crafted conclusion contains three components: a concise review, a specific request, and a tangible reward.

The Finished Product

As you probably already know, my last name is Rodriguez. That name reflects my Puerto Rican descent, but I am mostly Italian. I was raised with a strong Italian influence, and my fondest childhood memories are times spent at my Auntie Rosetta's and Uncles Angelo and Mario's house in Richmond, California. The Ricci family impacted my life in huge ways, particularly when it came to food. Every meal was an extravaganza. Auntie Rosetta would start preparing dinner in mid-morning and then she would cook all day with my uncles adding their unique culinary touches. The results were the best meals ever. Because of this experience, as an adult, my expectations related to food are quite high. As you can imagine, I'm not a big fan of potlucks.

When I met my wife, Colette, she was an average cook. Now she cooks like a gourmet chef. Over the years, it has been interesting to watch her develop her culinary skills. I noticed three things that characterize her development. First, she learned to follow recipes to the letter. Second, she watched the Food Network and learned from skilled chefs. Third, she started experimenting with her own recipes.

Speakers can learn a lot from the developmental path my wife took. As a novice speaker, it is good to follow a recipe, like the one I am giving you here. In addition, make sure you spend time studying speakers who are more proficient and polished than you. As you grow in knowledge and experience as a speaker, experiment until you find a comfortable style and technique that works for you.

Although it has taken us some time, you now have all the ingredients necessary to put together great talks. Given that we have examined all the components of a purpose-centered presentation, it's time to see what the finished product looks like.

Unfortunately, the only way to show you this example here is by using a manuscript, which is not my preferred method. However, it will serve our purposes. The following talk is illustrative and highlights the fundamentals we have covered so far. To begin, I've answered the four vital questions that were discussed in Chapter 2:

1. To whom am I speaking? My audience is a midsize gathering of male leaders between 40–60 years old. They lead organizations engaged in business and education. I am one of five speakers.

2. How much time do I have to speak? I have been given ten minutes to speak and ten minutes for practicum.

3. What subject will I be addressing? My subject is the value of shared vision in an organization. My title is: "What Vision Does for An Organization." My approach will be deductive.

4. What is my desired outcome? At the conclusion of my talk I will ask participants to write out a vision statement for their organization. They will also be asked to gather their key leaders within two weeks and solicit their feedback and input. The final goal is to draft and adopt a clearly defined vision statement that reflects the shared vision of the organization's leadership.

Special Note: Please notice the bracketed comments throughout the presentation, which are designed to point out specific features within the talk.

MODEL MESSAGE:
"WHAT VISION DOES FOR AN ORGANIZATION"

[Introduction] *Good morning! It is a great honor for me to be in the company of so many extraordinary leaders.* **[Introduction element: get the audience's attention →]** *Let's begin this morning with a short demonstration. I would like all of you to stand to your feet. Now, please close your eyes, no peeking! OK, with your eyes closed, I would like you to point north. Keep pointing north, but now, open your eyes and look around. Notice that people are pointing in a lot of different*

131

directions. That is because all of you have your own idea about which way is north. I brought a compass with me today to show you where north really is. The compass says north is this way. Thanks for playing along; now, please take a seat.

Organizations without clearly defined vision force leaders to figure a lot out on their own. Unfortunately, just as we saw in our little demonstration, that can lead to confusion, and even chaos. Vision is to an organization what a compass is to a navigator. Both serve to set the course and guide us along the way. **[Introduction essential: surface a need →]** *A clearly defined vision is fundamental to an organization's success. The reason is simply that, without vision, organizations lack a sense of purpose and direction. Why does your organization exist? What is its purpose and ultimate goal? Sooner or later, your leaders and team members will need to know the answers to these fundamental questions. (Sooner is always better than later when it comes to defining your organization's vision.)*

Now, let's look at an example of a vision statement from a company well known to us all, McDonald's:

> *"McDonald's vision is to be the world's best quick-service restaurant experience. Being the best means providing outstanding quality, service, cleanliness, and value, so that we make every customer in every restaurant smile."*

Often, I am asked the difference between a "vision statement" and a "mission statement." This is a great question that is fairly simple to answer. A vision statement focuses on an organization's purpose and future.

132

It looks forward to the company's long-term goals and objectives. On the other hand, a mission statement describes what an organization is currently doing related to their products, services, and customers. Vision highlights what an organization aspires to become in the future, whereas mission describes what that organization wants to achieve in the present. Obviously, both vision and mission are important. However, for our purposes here, our focus is exclusively on vision.

[Key questions that point to the desired outcome →] *Does your organization have a clearly defined vision? If I asked your leaders to recite your vision statement, could they do it? Or would their answers be as varied as the pointing north exercise in our demonstration earlier?*

The Harvard Business Review says, "Vision is a concise statement that defines the mid-to long-term (three- to 10-year) goals of the organization. [...] The stretch goal in the vision statement should truly be a difficult reach for the company in its present position". [7]

If an organization intends to succeed, developing a vision is not an option; it's a necessity. History proves that organizations without vision are destined for mediocrity and/or failure. This is true because, without vision, people waste a lot of time marching in place, or even worse, running in circles. On the other hand, organizations with a defined vision set their people up for success by providing them with a sense of purpose and a clearly stated objective.

---

7 Harvard Business Review, January 2008, Leadership & Strategy pg. 66

[The subject clearly stated in the introduction→] *It is important to understand what vision does for an organization. Vision gives an organization some distinct advantages, and over the next few minutes, I will highlight three of them. These advantages provide fundamental building blocks that promote success and foster organizational alignment.*

[Point listeners to desired outcome →] *My ultimate goal today is to encourage you and your team to clearly define your organization's vision. This involves a two-step process that I will talk more about later. For now, let us look at one advantage that vision gives to your organization.*

[End of introduction begins movement one →] *First, vision instills purpose. As a young boy, I recall sitting in front of a black-and-white television and seeing President John F. Kennedy announce his ambitious vision of sending an American to the moon by the end of the decade. Pressured by advances in the former Soviet Union's space program, Kennedy decided to enter the "space race." After talks with NASA's Administrator and other officials, he decided that landing an American on the moon would be technologically challenging, but possible. President Kennedy's vision gave NASA a new sense of purpose and definitive stretch goal. His vision set that huge organization in motion to achieve a historic milestone in space travel. On July 20, 1969, his grand goal was achieved when Apollo 11 commander Neil Armstrong stepped off the Lunar Module's ladder and onto the moon's surface. It all began with a vision.* **[End illustration]**

Vision in an organization instills a sense of purpose. Without purpose, motivating people is nearly impossible. A few years ago, Rick Warren wrote a great book entitled The Purpose-Driven Life. *I highly recommend you read it. The book became a national best seller in no time. Why? The answer is simple. Everyone is interested in living a purposeful life. The same is true when it comes to our work. It is much easier to motivate employees when we can show them that what they are doing matters. Very few people want to spend a third of their time working for a company that has no vision and, therefore, no purpose. Bill Hybels, founding and senior pastor of one of the most attended churches in North America, says, "Motivated employees are 87 percent less likely to leave an organization compared to an unmotivated employee."*

[Restate movement one →] *Vision instills purpose, and purpose motivates teams to work together. Arguably, one of the most coveted trophy in sports is hockey's Stanley Cup. A while back, I watched the San Jose Sharks (my home team) defeat the Detroit Red Wings in a fierce hockey series and move on to the Western Conference Finals, where they took a giant step toward winning the cup. Unfortunately, in the ensuing series, the Chicago Blackhawks, who went on to win the championship, knocked out the Sharks. Every season, players from all over the world have visions of winning the grand prize. They literally fight to win the right to hoist Lord Stanley's Cup over their heads in victory. This perennial vision instills a sense of purpose in players and motivates them to work together in hope of taking*

135

home this coveted prize. Vision instills purpose, and, in this case, purpose motivates players to overcome injury, adversity, and fierce competition in order to realize their dream. A clearly defined vision can instill purpose in your organization. When people are driven by purpose, it is amazing what they can accomplish.

[Begin the transition from movement one to movement two →] *The first advantage that vision gives to an organization is a purpose. Creating a sense of purpose for your employees and/or volunteers is fundamental to success.*

[Begin movement two →] *It is important to realize that vision not only instills purpose, it inspires passion — the second advantage that vision gives to your organization.*

[Begin illustration →] *The Susan G. Komen foundation is a vision-driven organization named after a woman who died of breast cancer 28 years ago. For almost three decades, this global organization has been committed to finding a cure for breast cancer. What you might not know is that the vision for this organization did not originate with Susan. Instead, it came from her sister, Nancy G. Brinker. Nancy promised her dying sister Susan that she would do everything within her power to end breast cancer forever. Subsequently, in 1982, Nancy's vision birthed the purpose-oriented organization known as "Susan G. Komen for the Cure."*

Since then this group has launched a global breast cancer movement, investing nearly $1.5 billion dollars in the fight against breast cancer during the past 28 years. The organization grew out of one woman's vision *to end this hideous disease, once and for all; yet today, thousands of passionate volunteers perpetuate the vision of this life-saving movement.*

[Restate movement two →] *Vision is what inspires passion. You are all organizational leaders. Although your organizations vary in size, they all have this in common. They all need a vision and leaders that are passionate about seeing that vision realized. Therefore, it is imperative that your leaders know your vision, and are passionate about seeing it achieved. When the leaders in your organization are given the opportunity to help craft your vision, their passions are stirred.*

Collective passion among your leaders can be infectious. Purpose coupled with passion can generate powerful momentum in your organization, but keep in mind that the level of passion within your organization will never be higher than your own level of passion.

In my business experience, I have observed two distinct types of leaders. One might be called the "pioneer," and the other, the "rancher." Pioneers are passionate about starting things up. They love to plow fresh ground and blaze new trails while ranchers are passionate about making the fields grow. They settle in for the long haul. Ranchers develop the land that pioneers discover. They enjoy turning wild territory into a thriving homestead.

I have come to believe that pioneers are lousy ranchers, and ranchers generally make equally bad pioneers. Occasionally you will find a leader that can both pioneer and ranch well, but this is truly rare.

I figured out a long time ago that I'm a pioneer. I love starting things up and/or turning things around. My passions are stirred by new challenges and fresh opportunities. I have also discovered that my passion quickly wanes when I find myself unwittingly slipping into the role of a rancher.

Years ago I managed a radio station in Kansas City for five years. When I first came to town the task at hand was to turn around the station's poor ratings. This took a couple of years of hard work and solid team effort. Once the initial goal was achieved, we spent the next couple years fighting back the competition. After being at the station about four years, I started to notice my passion and energy level were beginning to diminish. I found myself getting increasingly bored and listless with each passing day. I also noticed something else. My waning passion was reflected in a reduced zeal in those around me, and my declining passion was clearly beginning to adversely impact the organization. Eventually, I realized that the radio station needed a good rancher and I needed a new challenge. Passion is infectious, and so is a lack of it. Visionary leaders are responsible for bringing both purpose and passion to their organization.

[Transition statement: from movement two to movement three →] *Once again, I want to ask you a very important question: Do your leaders know your vision, and do they share your passion for it? Passion is another advantage that vision gives to an organization, but there is still one more advantage.*

[Begin movement three →] *Vision not only instills purpose and inspires passion, vision increases productivity—the third advantage that vision gives to your organization.*

[Begin illustration →] *We all know that enhanced productivity is a key ingredient to success. A few years ago, my wife and I went on a European cruise where we traveled from Amsterdam to the south and ended up in Spain. It was an incredible twelve-day trip. During our time away, we lounged around and ate and drank way too much. We noticed that part of the crew on the cruise ship was there to make sure the ship sailed on course and on time. The rest of the crew members ensured that the passengers' needs were well met. In essence, the passengers were along for the ride to relax, play, and indulge. However, not all big ships are cruise ships.*

A couple of years ago, a dear friend of mine told me that he had a chance to tour an active battleship stationed in Hawaii. There were no passengers lounging in deck chairs or waiters hawking piña coladas. Quite the opposite. On a battleship, the overall purpose is clear, and every person has an important assignment. These dedicated sailors are passionate and productive.

Vision bolsters productivity because it helps define the overall objective and clarify individual roles **[Key question →]** *Is your organization more like a cruise ship or a battleship? Are your employees along for the ride? Are they primarily focused on what they can get from your organization? This is a cruise ship mentality. If that is the case, your organization's productivity will suffer. However, if your team knows and embraces*

*your vision, has clearly defined roles, and a purpose-
ful assignment, they will function more like sailors on
a battleship. Suffice it to say that vision increases productivity, and increased productivity leads to organizational success and higher profits.*

[Transition into conclusion] *By now I hope you
agree that every organization can benefit from a clearly
defined vision, one that is known and embraced by its
leaders and team members.*

[Begin conclusion] *This morning we have looked
at three advantages that vision gives to an organization.*
[Conclusion element one: concise review] *Let's
review those advantages: First, vision instills purpose.
Second, vision inspires passion. Third, vision increases
productivity. When these fundamentals are in place, an
organization has a solid foundation on which to build.*

*Today, I want to share with you two organizational
success stories. The first one comes from the field of education, the second from the world of business. Both exemplify what vision does for an organization. My first
example is a school on the South Side of Chicago. As
most of you probably already know, Chicago's South
Side is notorious for gangs, violence, and drugs. In this
tough section of the city, many young black men lose
their way. Sadder still, too many others lose their lives.
But in the midst of this dangerous and difficult environment, there is a charter school named Urban Prep
Academy, a school that is the vision of an education
entrepreneur named Tim King. His vision for Urban
Prep is "to provide a comprehensive, high-quality college preparatory education to young men that results*

140

in graduates succeeding in college." According to the school's website, this is "a direct response to the urgent need to reverse abysmal graduation and college completion rates among young men in urban centers, particularly African-American males." "We Believe" is the Urban Prep motto:

"We believe that our students will shatter negative stereotypes and defy low expectations. We believe that our students can be prepared for and will succeed in college. We believe in the long-lasting impact that community support and positive role models can have on our students' lives. In short, we believe in our students' futures. At Urban Prep, we believe."[8]

This inspirational vision has instilled purpose, inspired passion, and increased student productivity, so much so that in May 2008, ABC's Good Morning America *reported an incredible and unprecedented occurrence. All 107 senior students at Urban Prep Academy were accepted into four-year colleges. This is a remarkable achievement that all began with one man's vision—a vision that instilled purpose, inspired passion, and increased productivity in a group of students surrounded by dangerous and difficult circumstances.*

My second example comes from the world of business. One of my specialties as a consultant is senior level conflict resolution. When I was brought into a nationally known insurance agency in the Silicon Valley, my assignment was to resolve a conflict within the leadership team. After a few meetings, the conflict was

8 www.urbanprep.org

resolved and cooler heads prevailed. During my assignment there I worked closely with the agency's owner. In working with her, I discovered the agency was lacking vision, values, a strategic plan, and ways to measure growth, except for a few sales metrics. To shorten a long story, the owner subsequently hired me to help her develop vision, values, a strategic plan, and practical metrics for measuring the growth and development of her business and personnel. After a couple of meetings, we crafted a proposed vision and shared it with her team. They contributed helpful input, and the shared vision was agreed upon and adopted. The vision instilled a new sense of purpose, passion, and productivity in her team. A short while later, the owner of the agency sent me an email informing me that her agency tied for fifth place in generating new business out of sixty-five other agencies in the area. To say the least, she was elated. Once again, it all started with a clearly defined vision.

*Now it is your turn. After my concluding remarks, you will be given an exercise and a challenge. [***Conclusion element two: a specific request →***] What you'll be doing is taking a first pass at crafting a vision statement for your organization. If you already have a vision statement, you can utilize this time to reexamine it.*

After you complete the vision statement, commit to sharing it with your leadership team within the next two weeks. In doing this, solicit their feedback and ask for their input. This will help you develop a shared vision that your leaders will own with you.

**[Conclusion element three: a tangible reward
➔]** *In conclusion, I am convinced that all of you want to instill purpose, inspire passion, and increase productivity within your individual organizations. Vision will help you do just that.*

Thanks so much for giving me the honor and privilege of sharing my thoughts on vision with you today. Why does your organization exist? And what are you hoping to accomplish? You now have ten minutes to take a stab at answering those questions, so let's get started! **[This concludes the illustrative talk.]**

Well there you have it! You now have a proven way for preparing a talk. Obviously, with time and practice you will develop your own "customized" approach. For now, however, use this model message as a general guide to make sure your presentations are purpose-centered, your structure is hidden, and your key components support your desired outcome. This will definitely improve your ability to communicate more effectively and ensure that your messages impact your listening audience.

Preparing a good talk is one thing; delivering it in an effective way is quite another. In the next and final chapter, you will learn how to improve your speaking mannerisms and delivery techniques.

Purpose-Centered Public Speaking
PREPARATION GUIDE »》 VISUAL PROCESS

FOUR VITAL QUESTIONS
To whom am I speaking?
How much time do I have to speak?
What subject will I be addressing?
What is my desired outcome?

IDENTIFY A SINGLE SUBJECT

DETERMINE A DESIRED OUTCOME
What will you be asking the audience to do at the end of your talk?

CHOOSE SPEECH TYPE

SELECT A STRUCTURE
(Manuscript, full outline, movements, key words, etc.)

DETERMINE A TEACHING METHOD
(Inductive, deductive, or another approach.)

CRAFT YOUR INTRODUCTION

DECIDE ON POINTED ILLUSTRATIONS

FORMULATE A CONCLUSION

144

CHAPTER 10

Presentation Tips

"ACT THE WAY YOU'D LIKE TO BE AND
SOON YOU'LL BE THE WAY YOU ACT."
– George W. Crane

My goal throughout this book has been to present and demonstrate a simple, purposeful, and systematic approach to public speaking. Consequently, we have talked a lot about developing the presentation. Now it is time to talk briefly about skills and techniques helpful in delivering it. Although I feel obligated to touch on this subject, it is impossible to do it justice in one chapter. Therefore, my hope is that you will refer to the resources I've included in this chapter and elsewhere in the book.

Good presentation skills and techniques are an essential part of effective public speaking, so it's time to look at four broad categories: Appearance, Body Language, Voice and Tone, and Audience Connection.

Appearance

When it comes to public speaking, first impressions matter. In many cases, the speaker is a stranger to the audience. Initially, the only way for an audience to evaluate a speaker is by their visual appearance. Many of us know the expression, "don't judge a book by its cover," but that is exactly what most of us do. Think about your last trip to a bookstore. You entered the store and found the aisle housing the books that interested you. Then, most likely, you browsed through the shelves for a title or cover that captured your attention. Once you saw it, you picked up the book and looked inside. Countless numbers of good books go unread because of uninteresting titles, or downright boring covers. When it comes to speaking, your appearance is like a book cover, and it really does matter.

Several years ago, I mentored a female speaker who had an above average gift of communication. Her challenge was that she did not know how to groom or dress when speaking. Often, she would show up for presentations looking disheveled with unbrushed hair. Her appearance put people off, particularly other women. It was clearly a distraction that took away from her credibility and message. Her shabby appearance distracted her audience and minimized her effectiveness. After a few delicate conversations, she started paying more careful attention to her appearance and discovered the importance of preparing not only her message, but also herself. In time, she learned to eliminate the physical distractions that had been working against her.

Experienced speakers recognize that, prior to speaking, it's a good idea to look at yourself in the mirror. Unfortunately, several years ago, I learned this lesson the hard way. A few minutes into my talk, I noticed a young man in the front row making peculiar gestures at me. His left hand was low in front of his chest. With the index finger and thumb of his right hand, he was feverishly making an up and down

Presentation Tips:
- *www.aresearchguide.com/3tips.html*
- *www2.fpm.wisc.edu/support/PresentationTips.htm*
- *www.garrreynolds.com/Presentation/index.html*
- *www.speech-topics-help.com*

Books on Presenting:
- The Short Road to Great Presentations—How to Reach Any Audience Through Focused Preparation, Inspired Delivery, and Smart Use of Technology, *by Cheryl Reimond and Peter Reimond (Wiley, 2003)*
- Presenting to Win—The Art of Telling Your Story, *by Jerry Weissman (FT Press, 2008). (How to transform your presentations from dry recitals of facts into compelling stories with a laser-sharp focus on what matters most: what's in it for your audience.)*
- Do Not Go Naked into Your Next Presentation—Nifty Little Nuggets to Quiet the Nerves and Please the Crowd, *by Ron Hoff (Andrews MeMeel Pub., 1997)*

motion. Finally, in a desperate attempt to get his message across, he pointed to his zipper. Suddenly, I realized that my zipper was open. (Earlier, when talking about the introduction, I talked about getting the audience's attention. I do not recommend this method). I quickly glided over to the lectern and zipped up my pants, to the delight of an anxious and distracted audience. Please learn by wisdom what I learned by consequence, and always take the time to examine yourself in front of a full-length mirror before you hit the podium.

Another important consideration is related to what

you choose to wear. Some believe it is smart to dress slightly better than your audience, but I do not recommend this. In most cases, I believe it is a better idea to match the dress of your audience. This does not necessarily mean mimicking their style. Instead, think in terms of matching their degree of formality or lack thereof. Here in the Silicon Valley, it is generally unwise to dress up in a suit and tie to speak to a group of mid-level managers. If you do, you will probably be way overdressed.

When I spoke in Portland, Oregon to a group of senior executives at a company's annual meeting, almost all the men were wearing jeans. Some wore just a shirt while others wore jackets. I wore jeans and a casual shirt and sport coat and fit right in. All this is to say that you need to pay attention to how you look. Do not give your audience any reason to turn you off before you say anything.

Body Language

We speak with more than just words. Our body has a silent language of its own that reveals our temperament, attitude, and disposition. Thus the speaker's body language can either aid or hinder the audience's receptivity to the spoken word. Here, body language refers to the presenter's general demeanor, gestures, posture, and eye movement. Consider first the speaker's general demeanor.

General Demeanor. Several years ago, while traveling out of state, I visited a new church on a Sunday morning. After a time of worship, the pastor got up to speak. Minutes into his sermon, it seemed like he was mad at his congregation.

He was tense and came across angry and extremely frustrated. His message was scolding, and he seemed irritated by the people in the pews. To make matters worse, his subject that morning was on "loving one another." It was sheer courtesy that kept me from walking out. I heard what he had to say, but I found it neither credible nor believable. His general demeanor betrayed him. In all fairness, maybe he wasn't mad at the congregation at all. Perhaps he'd had a fight with his wife that morning or something else was troubling him. Whatever the reason, his general disposition negated the message of love he was trying to convey. Remember this story the next time you hit the podium, because your general demeanor can either serve you or sink you.

Gestures. Used properly, gestures can add to your presentation. There are three basic types: those used for emphasis, those used to describe something that cannot be physically seen, and those that serve as pointers.

- *EMPHASIS* gestures involve the use of your body to highlight a particular word, point, or movement in the message. This is often done with hand movements and or by leaning into the audience for effect.

- *IMAGE* gestures are used to describe something to the audience that they cannot physically see. For instance, you might use your hands and arms to show how skinny a person is, or how big the dog was that tried to bite you. It is helpful to consider how you might use your hands and arms

149

to describe the above examples without saying a word. Your goal is to help the audience see something that is not present.

• *POINTING GESTURES* are used when the speaker needs to point something out to the audience that he wants them to look at; for example, pointing at something on a screen. If you like to use PowerPoint or visual aids, you will use this gesture a lot to direct the audience's attention to something you want to show them.

There are many other types of gestures but these three are the most commonly used. A word of caution, however. Do not overuse gestures because they can be very distracting to listeners if they are used too much or at the wrong times. The best gestures are natural and in sync with the words being spoken. Avoid bad gestures such as pointing too much at the audience, nervous hand habits, hands in pockets, or folding your arms while speaking. The best way to improve and break bad habits is by watching videos of your presentations since this will highlight both your strengths and challenges related to gesturing. As you will discover, the more you speak, the more natural your gestures will become.

Posture. The next aspect of body language involves *posture*. The Presenters' Blog says, "There are three things your hands should avoid touching during a presentation; your chest, your hips, and each other! [...] When we feel insecure, we use defensive body postures. [...] The optimal posture for presenters is to keep the upper body 'open'; free from defensive body postures."[9]

This is great advice. Open posture indicates a relaxed, comfortable, and confident presenter. Standing up straight and keeping your posture open clears the way for your audience to see and hear you. Let me say again, watch yourself on video and keep an eye on your posture throughout your presentation. Good posture and good communication go hand in hand.

Eye Movement. Another aspect of body language is *eye movement*. Eye contact helps personalize the message to the audience, and good eye contact can make individuals in the audience feel as though you are talking just to them. Eye contact should not be forced but natural. Unlike the presenter who feels obligated to make eye contact with everyone in the audience, the wise presenter is selective. He or she naturally moves from person to person, establishing a short but powerful connection. Eye contact that is unnatural can make audience members feel uncomfortable. Darting eyes and jerky head movements can be very distracting during a presentation, so learn to break eye contact in a natural way. Usually this means at the end of a sentence or a point.

Avoid focusing on the same person too long. How do you know when it is too long? When the person you are looking at goes from "glad you spotted me," to "wish you would stop staring at me," you have stayed with the same person too long. Eventually, with more experience, you will get a feel for "appropriate" eye contact. For now, remember

9 http://speak2all.wordpress.com/2009/04/27/presentation-body-language-hands-and-open-posture/

that good eye contact with the audience is important, but a judicious use of it is equally important.

Facial Expressions. Here's a final thought related to the use of body language; namely, the importance of your *facial expressions,* which send out powerful messages to your audience. Inappropriate facial expressions can actually derail a presentation. For example, if you are speaking about a serious subject with a smirk on your face, this will confuse the audience and impede your message. On the other hand, if you are saying something humorous, but aren't smiling when you say it, that can be a bit disconcerting to your listeners. Generally, the nature and tone of your words should match your facial expressions. If they do not, there should be a good reason for it. Use your face to animate your words, or, if you prefer, do it the other way around.

Voice and Tone

Voice. In this context, *voice* refers to the way we use our physical vocal abilities, while tone refers to "how" and with "what" intonation we say something. First, here are some tips on how to strengthen your voice.

There are many tools and practical helps available when it comes to improving your voice quality. The following is a summary of some free and simple tips that can help you improve the resonance and clarity of your voice. (My thanks to Beth J. Mann, whose article on EzineArticles.com [see article link below] discusses the following tips in greater detail).[10]

1. Practice humming. This exercise helps promote a more natural sound and placement of your voice. Experts suggest humming for at least five minutes before speaking.

2. Yawn more often. This may sound silly, but yawning opens up your voice, thus improving its sound quality. When yawning, do it out loud. Try to simulate a noisy yawn even when it is not natural, because this exercise will open up the back of your throat.

3. Bray like a donkey. Yes, the secret is to imitate the braying sound of a donkey. This useful exercise helps you develop a relaxed but forceful voice. For help with learning to bray, visit the footnote link below, (or talk to someone you think acts like a jackass).

4. Work on your annunciation. Most of us are lazy when it comes to the way we speak, particularly when it comes to pronouncing our T's. Work on careful annunciation to improve your diction and promote clarity. (No more "budder," please; the word is "butter.")

5. Allow your words to breathe. Many of us have a tendency to run words together. One tip here is to practice exaggerating each word. This will help

10 http://ezinearticles.com/?quick-and-easy-ways-to-Improve-your-speaking-voice&id=860389

train your mouth and tongue to articulate each word. In time, this will help you break bad speech patterns.

6. Learn from the pros: Whenever you get a chance, listen to great communicators. Notice their clear pronunciation and the way they articulate their words. Take time to practice speaking slowly and clearly in front of a mirror. Get used to what it feels like to articulate words properly.

7. Breathing. Good breathing is the foundation of a strong speaking voice. Breathing deeply can improve your ability to speak from your abdomen and greatly improve the quality of your voice.

Tone. Now that we've covered the topic of voice, it's time to focus on its companion, tone. A little story will help you understand its importance. My son Paul lives in Michigan. Because I live in California, we do not have much in-person time, so we talk on the phone quite a bit. During our calls, we talk about all kinds of things. One part of these calls always involves my son giving me an update on my granddaughter, Addison. I love it when he talks about the "little pickle," and I delight in hearing him speak with such tender emotion about her. His words reveal the strong emotional bond he has with her. Since he feels so much love for Addison, would it not be odd if he spoke about her in a "matter-of-fact tone"? In other words, what if he spoke about her as if he had no emotional attachment to her? That would be not only strange, but his profession of love for her would sound hollow, empty, and void of emotion.

The voice displays emotion through vocal tones, thus a speaker's "disposition and mood" toward a subject are plainly exposed by the tone of his or her voice. In fact, a speaker's inflections can radically change the tenor and meaning of a statement. For example, if I say, "Don't be late," the way I say it can either sound "suggestive" (try not to be late), or "dictatorial" (you had better not to be late). Like facial expressions, tone reveals how speakers are feeling about what they are saying. In hearing one speaker, you might say, "he spoke in a harsh tone." In referring to another, you might say there was "an encouraging tone about her message."

Since presentations have both a general tone and a variety of specific tonal inflections throughout, it's always important to think about what general tone you would like to characterize your message. Does the content call for a general tone that is humorous, friendly, serious, business-like, cautionary, encouraging or something else? You can be sure that the tonal inflections throughout your message will come naturally if you remain emotionally connected to the words you are speaking. Nevertheless, it is always a good idea to think about the general presentation tone you would prefer to convey.

Most of us have heard speakers that appear to be emotionally disconnected from their content. Their unnatural tone betrays them, and the audience is left wondering how much they care about what they are saying. Passionate presenters, however, are emotionally connected to their content and portray a deep level of investment in their subject. These speakers help us to not only *hear* their message, but *feel* it as well. While the level of passion one shows is directly tied to the nature of the subject matter, a passionate speaker can invigorate even a dry subject.

A while back, I heard a talk chronicling the lifelong damage that child abuse does to its victims. The speaker was herself a survivor of child abuse. Although she was not a polished speaker, her emotional connection to her content made her message both poignant and powerful. Audiences cut a lot of slack to novice presenters when they speak from the heart. Strong passion is no substitute for good content, but it certainly can help ingratiate a speaker to the audience.

As discussed earlier, the vocal tone and inflections within your message ought to match the mood of the words you are speaking. If a speaker is talking about something serious, it is obviously inappropriate to be smiling and talking in a jovial tone. The exception to this is when a technique is being used by design for a specific effect, (i.e., humor). Conversely, if a speaker is telling a joke but looks overly serious or talks in an angry tone, the joke will most likely fall flat.

The meaning of our words automatically influences the tone of our voice. Whenever our tone mirrors our content, our speech sounds natural and believable. However, when it does not, we tend to sound insincere and robot-like. Do you remember *Star Trek*, a long-running TV show that eventually became a series of popular movies? There was a character on the show, a Vulcan named Mr. Spock. He played a fictional character that lacked emotion, but made up for it with superior intellect. He was famous for speaking without showing the slightest emotional connection to what he was saying. Unfortunately, over the years, I have sat through some "Spock-like" presentations. They are never

156

enjoyable because the mismatch between tone and content makes the presentation look and sound inauthentic. Always remember that audiences are not "tone" deaf. They will intuitively monitor your tone throughout your presentation. If your feelings are married to your words, your tone will be natural and in tune with your listeners. If they are not, don't be surprised if your new nickname is Spock.

Audience Connection

Audience connection is an essential aspect of an effective presentation, and its importance cannot be overstated. Connecting to an audience creates a bridge over which content flows. Failure to connect with the audience will limit the impact of even the best-prepared messages.

Many of you have seen or at least heard of the hit television show, "So You Think You Can Dance." The show's popularity is tied to its ability to discover, develop, and showcase young aspiring dancers. I recall a show where one of the judges was critiquing a dance performance. In essence, he said that well choreographed dances tend to fall flat if the dancers fail to connect with their audience. Dancers do not have the benefit of words to create audience connection, and neither do mimes. Both use music, facial and body movements, choreographed gestures, emotional projection, and acting skills to draw in an audience.

Presenters are wise to think like dancers and mimes when it comes to connecting with an audience. Besides your words, how can you connect with the audience? Again, practicing in front of a mirror is the key here. Begin by standing in front of a full-length mirror and watch yourself try to convey that you are hungry without any words. What does your face look like? What gestures help convey that you are hungry?

Then try to convey that you feel full after a big meal. How would you show someone you were feeling full? Again, what are your face and eyes saying? What gestures or movements will you use? The more you learn to communicate short messages non-verbally, the more natural your stage gestures will become. There are literally thousands of scenarios you can attempt to convey in front of a mirror. After practicing without words for a while, add words back into the equation. In time, you will learn to show your audience what you are saying, not just tell them. Of course, like anything, this can be overdone. The ultimate goal is to develop fluid movements that are in sync with the nature of the words you are speaking.

Barriers to Connection. Before talking about three factors that promote audience connection, let's look at some obstacles that hinder it. In John Maxwell's book, *Everyone Communicates, Few Connect—What the Most Effective People Do Differently*,[11] he emphasizes four barriers that obstruct connection, namely:

1. **Assumption:** "I Already Know What Others Know, Feel, and Want"

2. **Arrogance:** "I Don't Need to Know What Others Know, Feel, or Want"

---

11 John Maxwell, Everyone Communicates, Few Connect (Thomas Nelson, 2010), 125-131

3. **Indifference:** "I Don't Care to Know What Others Know, Feel, or Want"

4. **Control:** "I Don't Want Others to Know What I Know, Feel, or Want"

Each barrier is reflective of a counterproductive belief and/or attitude in the speaker that breaks audience connection. Maxwell's book is a "must-read" for both aspiring and veteran speakers, one that is rich in content and written from his vast reservoir of knowledge and experience. The barriers he highlights are very common mistakes that must be avoided if speakers hope to find common ground with an audience.

Three Keys to Connecting with an Audience. The keys to connecting with an audience involve speakers making some intentional commitments. Think of them as three key commitments that foster connection. They promote an audience-centered approach and pave the way for developing common ground. This approach puts the needs of the audience first, and reveals the speaker's intention to "give," not "take" from an audience.

My consulting company, LeaderMetrix, specializes in senior-level executive coaching and conflict resolution. Generally, we are hired by a board of directors to work with a gifted senior leader on issues related to their ongoing development. During some of these engagements we support leaders interested in further developing their recognized strengths. We also assist leaders in shoring up some personal and/or relational challenge(s) adversely impacting their organization.

159

When we come into an organization, the initial meeting is designed to show the leader we are there to serve them. This means providing them with tools that will help them help themselves. The same is true with audiences. Speakers must show they are there to serve the audience and provide them with something of value. Connecting with an audience happens when speakers are committed to helping their audiences experience all three of the following:

1. A Relevant Encounter
2. A Reciprocal Exchange
3. A Rewarding Experience

A Relevant Encounter. The first key to connecting with the audience is "a relevant encounter." As stated previously, relevance describes speaking about something that matters to an audience. As obvious as this may sound, it does not always happen. Speakers can easily be driven by their own wants, rather than by an audience's interests and needs. Messages can quickly become more about serving the speaker than serving the audience.

In order to create a relevant encounter, speakers must spend time understanding the circumstances and needs of their listening audience. As emphasized earlier, the more speakers know about their audience, the better chance they will have of scratching listeners where they are itching. See *Audience Analysis Questionnaire* in the Appendix.

Many years ago I attended a conference on personal development with about three hundred other men. At the core of the conference, there were opportunities to attend both joint sessions and breakout workshops. On one

160

particular afternoon there were three breakout workshops being offered at the same time. One of them was on "Better Budgeting," a second focused on "Developing a Healthy Lifestyle," and the third was on "Breaking Free from the Grip of Pornography." Curious to know where the men were itching, I waited ten minutes after we were dismissed to the workshops. I discovered that both the "Better Budgeting" and "Healthy Lifestyle" breakout rooms had only about ten men in attendance. No question about where these men were itching. When I walked down the hall to the designated room for the "Breaking Free from the Grip of Pornography" workshop, everyone was going in the opposite direction. When I inquired what was going on, I was told that the original room could not hold the crowd of men wanting to attend the workshop, and everyone was being relocated to the main conference room. Now *that* is what you call a relevant message!

Perhaps you have heard the often-used expression, "You are preaching to the choir." The expression describes talking to an audience about something they already know or possess. In other words, telling an audience something they do not need to know or want to hear. In the eyes of the audience, this is an irrelevant message. Talks that lack relevance are quickly dismissed as a waste of time, but a relevant message is one that taps

> *A relevant encounter begins with a speaker's commitment to serve the audience first. Part of a presenter's fundamental duty is to ensure that the audience has a meaningful experience, and this demands that our messages are both audience-centered and pertinent.*

161

into something that matters to listeners, fosters connection, and ingratiates the speaker to his or her audience.

A Reciprocal Exchange. The second key to connecting with the audience is "a reciprocal exchange" that results in "a shared experience." A shared experience is another way of saying that a transaction takes place between the speaker and his or her listening audience, one that involves an exchange of emotion and knowledge. Generally, audiences do not care how much we know until they know how much we care. Care is shown when a speaker can engage the audience on an emotional as well as informational level. This kind of exchange creates a bond that bolsters connection. Let me show you what I mean.

In speaking to a group about how to balance life's priorities, I did not begin by talking about the solution. Instead, I began by talking about the problem of pressing priorities that we all face. This approach helped the audience know that I felt the same kind of pressure they were also experiencing. This quickly enabled me to forge an emotional connection with everyone in the room and opened the door for me to share my insights on the subject with them. I could not assume they knew that I understood what they were thinking or feeling; I had to *show* them.

As you can see, a reciprocal exchange involves connecting on both an emotional as well as an intellectual level. When a speaker shares insights that resonate with the audience and reflect the listener's own experiences, another powerful exchange takes place. Insights about issues, struggles, problems, and difficulties associated with change and development give listeners a sense that we live in the same world they do. These shared insights create connection because they show the speaker's ability to relate to the audience's day-to-day reality. The more a speaker can identify with the audience, the greater credibility he or she will gain with their listeners.

Have you ever listened to a speaker and come to the conclusion that he or she "doesn't get it"? Such speakers seem otherworldly and not able to understand the struggles and challenges you face. They seem unwilling or unable to relate to you; therefore, you find it difficult to relate to them. To keep his students' feet on the ground, my professor, Dr. Haddon Robinson, used a great tool he called the "depravity factor." The depravity factor is that base part in us that opposes, resists, or struggles with what we know we can and should do. Throughout every message, I am always asking myself, "What is the audience opposing, resisting, or struggling with related to what I am saying?" Knowing this helps me address these issues head-on instead of bypassing or ignoring them. One way to do this is by using "leading questions."

Leading questions address the questions listeners are thinking about but are generally unable or too afraid to ask. Suppose a speaker made a statement like this: "Leaders must learn to develop the leaders they manage." If I were in the audience, I might be thinking, *sure that makes perfect sense, but how is that done?* The speaker should intuitively know that is what the audience is thinking. Why? The answer is simple, because if you, the speaker, were in the audience, that is most likely what you would be thinking. In the above example, a speaker might follow up the previous statement with a question such as: "Now you are probably

163

saying to yourself, yes, I do need to identify and develop the leaders around me, but how do I do it? Pay careful attention because that is the exact question I will be answering during the next few minutes."

Leading and pointed questions are great tools to use for keeping listeners engaged. Speakers are wise to continually anticipate the questions their audience wishes they could be asking. Answering listeners' silent questions will help keep the audience with you, while failure to anticipate and answer these questions is a sure way to lose their interest and attention.

A Rewarding Experience. The third key to connecting with the audience is making sure listeners have "a rewarding experience." This means that listeners must walk away with something of value. That is why the "desired outcome" we spoke about earlier is so important. The "desired outcome" helps the presenter predetermine the audience's "take away," and doing this requires advance planning to make certain that listeners leave with something of worth. This is what makes the time investment and whole experience rewarding for the audience. Ultimately, the things most listeners want to know are what's in it for them, how will the talk help them, and what will they take away at the end. Remember, the time to think about the value you intend to leave with your audience is not at the end but at the beginning of your preparation work (See "Beginning at the End"– Chapter 4). Even though this process takes time, in the end, it is well worth it, especially for the people who are positively impacted by your presentation.

By now, you understand the vital importance of connecting with an audience and may wish to do more study on the subject. Again, I urge you to read John Maxwell's book, *Everyone Communicates, Few Connect* because it is the best book I have read on this topic to date. It unpacks the subject in a masterful way and highlights what the most effective communicators do to connect with audiences. I know you will find it helpful.

> *Speakers that offer audiences a relevant encounter, a reciprocal exchange, and a rewarding experience, will find connecting much easier because the audience will sense you are there to serve them, not just yourself.*

Final Thoughts

I became the youngest drill sergeant in the history of the U.S. Army when I was eighteen years old. At the time, I was stationed at Ft. Knox, Kentucky. My job as a drill sergeant was to introduce new recruits to Army life and prepare them for possible deployment to Viet Nam. I took my job very seriously because I knew lives were at stake. When it comes to public speaking, there are also lives on the line. Words can influence people to do great or horrible things. Words can give life, or they can bring death.

Words are a lot like seeds. The nature of their source determines what they produce. Just as an apple seed produces an apple tree, an encouraging word can cultivate encouragement and a sense of hope. *Words have tremendous power.*

As public speakers, we have the awesome responsibility of using words that can build people up or tear them down. God forbid that we are ever guilty of doing the latter. My hope and prayer is that our words will make a positive impact on those who hear us speak. May our speech be encouraging and uplifting whenever possible. Let us sow hope where there is despair, plant love where there is hate, and bring light where there is darkness. In the end, people will be better or worse off because of what we convey. Therefore, let us speak as if we will be held accountable for every word, because, according to the Good Book, we will be.

Appendix

Fear of Public Speaking Phobia Test

Use this simple test to determine whether or not you have a serious fear of public speaking. Try to answer the questions honestly to obtain the most accurate results. It is recommended that you take this test when you are alone and in a quiet setting.

After taking the test, add up your scores and see whether you have a low, moderate, or severe fear of public speaking.

Low

Your fear of public speaking is low if your score is 15 points or below. You actually have no phobia. You experience a normal level of tension when you are in front of an audience. This level of anxiety can be overcome with breathing exercises and a good night's sleep. There is no cause for concern.

Moderate

If your score is between 16 to 45 points, join to the club! Like many people, you tend to feel very uncomfortable talking in front of a crowd. Nerves and tensions tend to influence your behavior in a more serious way. However, please do not despair. There are plenty of books, seminars, and online courses designed to help you overcome this kind of fear and anxiety. You will find page numbers for "Resources" listed in the Table of Contents.

Severe

If your score is over 45 points, you most likely suffer from the phobia fear of public speaking. You try to avoid any situation that might include public speaking. You hate making and/or giving presentations or speeches. It is extremely difficult for you to speak in front of a group. Even so, it is still possible to cure this phobia with some help and time. Check out the "Resources" pages in this book or visit www.speech-topics-help.com for more information.

Public Speaking Phobia Test

	never	rarely	sometimes	often	always
1. A tense and quivering voice	☐	☐	☐	☐	☐
2. Accelerated heart rate	☐	☐	☐	☐	☐
3. An overwhelming urge to flee the situation	☐	☐	☐	☐	☐
4. Cold hands	☐	☐	☐	☐	☐
5. Dizziness	☐	☐	☐	☐	☐
6. Dry mouth and/or throat	☐	☐	☐	☐	☐
7. Excessive blushing	☐	☐	☐	☐	☐
8. Feelings of self-doubt	☐	☐	☐	☐	☐
9. Feelings of uncertainty	☐	☐	☐	☐	☐
10. Thoughts like 'I'm embarrassing myself'	☐	☐	☐	☐	☐
11. Nervousness	☐	☐	☐	☐	☐
12. Rapid heart beat	☐	☐	☐	☐	☐
13. Negative thoughts of things going badly	☐	☐	☐	☐	☐
14. Shaky knees	☐	☐	☐	☐	☐
15. Sickness in the stomach	☐	☐	☐	☐	☐
16. Stammering	☐	☐	☐	☐	☐
17. Stuttering	☐	☐	☐	☐	☐
18. Sweaty hands	☐	☐	☐	☐	☐
19. Trembling hands	☐	☐	☐	☐	☐
20. Trembling lips	☐	☐	☐	☐	☐

Total Score:

Never = 0, Rarely = 1, Sometimes = 2, Often = 3, and Always = 4

Audience Analysis Questionnaire

The first vital question discussed in Chapter 2 asks, "To whom am I speaking?" Using this Audience Analysis Questionnaire will provide you with important demographic and psychographic details about your listeners. Remember, the more you know about your audience the better. Insights gained from the following questionnaire will help you shape your message to the audience. Keep in mind that this is a basic level questionnaire. Please feel free to add or delete questions in order to make this audience survey better suited to your situation.

It is helpful to get a completed audience analysis as early as possible in your preparation process. Consider emailing your questionnaire to your host as soon as you know you will be speaking somewhere.

1. Describe any special needs, problems, issues, or concerns currently facing this audience.

2. Describe the reason for this event and the amount of time participants will be engaged in it?

3. How much time will I have to speak, including Q&A and discussion time?

4. Approximately how many people will be in attending this event?

5. What percentage of the audience will be women _____? men _____?

6. What is the average age of the audience? _____

7. Will there be a heavier concentration of any particular age group? If yes, please describe them.

8. Will there be children or youth present? If yes, please highlight their genders and approximate ages.

9. What is your desired outcome from this event? In other words, what would you like the audience to walk away with as a result of attending this event?

10. Please tell me as much as you can about the kind of people I will be addressing. For instance, what are their occupations and professions? What is their average educational level? What is their average income level? Etc.

11. Describe anything else about the listening audience that will better prepare me to serve them.

12. Will there be any other presenters at this event? If yes, what subjects will they be addressing? Will I be speaking before or after them?

13. Do you have a particular subject in mind that you would like me to address? If so, please describe it in detail.

14. If I am free to choose my own topic, advise me on some themes that you think would be of interest to this audience.

15. Are there any subjects recently talked about or subjects that I should avoid?

16. Do you have any final thoughts or suggestions that will help me to make this a successful event?

Resources

Websites

www.toastmasters.org: *This nonprofit organization, which has nearly 260,000 members in over 12,500 clubs in 113 countries, offers proven and enjoyable ways to practice and hone communication and leadership skills.*

www.speakermatch.com/about.htm/ — *SpeakerMatch is an organization that matches speakers and speaking opportunities. It reaches emerging professional speakers, business leaders, technical gurus, educators, and other subject-matter experts who want to communicate what they know.*

www.ljlseminars.com/monthtip.htm/ — *Lenny Laskowski is an international professional speaker and an expert on presentation skills and related topics.*

www.history.com/speeches/ — *Famous speeches in history (Presidential, War, Civil Rights, Sports and Space Exploration).*

www.speech-topics-help.com/fear-of-public-speaking-phobia. html/ — *This site offers the "Fear of Public Speaking Self-Help Online Test" and a plethora of helps for speakers (highly recommended).*

www.speak4money.com/ — *Read the free articles on this site, and subscribe to Great Speaking Ezine, which contains hundreds of professional public speaking and presentation skills tips and tricks. (The ezine has its own website at GreatSpeaking.com. It claims to be the largest and most widely read Internet public speaking publication in the world, offering a wealth of FREE public speaking tips, tools, and secrets.)*

www.Tech4Speakers.com/ — *Helps speakers use technology more efficiently and more effectively—in their presentations, in office productivity, in marketing, product development, and in improving their online presence.*

www.communicateusingtechnology.com/ — *Here you will find PowerPoint Presentation tips and help in how to create persuasive visual presentations.*

Books

There's No Such Thing as Public Speaking—Make Any Presentation or Speech as Persuasive as a One-on-One Conversation, by Jeanette and Roy Henderson (Prentice Hall Press, 2007)

Public Speaking In An Instant–60 Ways to Stand Up and Be Heard (In an Instant), by Keith Bailey & Karen Leland (Career Press, 2009)

The Confident Speaker: Beat Your Nerves and Communicate At Your Best in Any Situation, by Harrison Monarth and Larina Kase (McGraw-Hill, 2007)

Dazzle 'Em With Style: The Art of Oral Scientific Presentations, by Robert R. H. Anholt (Academic Press, 2nd ed., 2005)

Confessions of A Public Speaker – Scott Berkun (O'Reilly Media, 2009)

Slide:ology: The Art and Science of Creating Great Presentations, by Nancy Duarte (O'Reilly Media, 2008)

Public Speaking: A Handbook for Christians – Duane A. Litfin (Baker Academic, 2nd ed., 1992)

Public Speaking Handbook, by Steven A. Beebe and Susan J. Bebee (Pearson, 2010)

The Power Presenter: Technique, Style, and Strategy from America's Top Speaking Coach, by Jerry Weissman (Wiley, 2009)

The Craft of Scientific Presentations: Critical Steps to Succeed and Critical Errors to Avoid, by Michael Alley (Springer, 2002)

Blogs[12]

Andrew Dlugan: Six Minutes
Twitter: @6minutes
This blog focuses on public speaking and presentation skills.

Lisa Braithwaite: Speak Schmeak
Twitter: @LisaBraithwaite
Lisa posts articles nearly every day, and she spreads words of encouragement through the public speaking blogosphere in article comments.

Bert Decker: Decker Blog
Twitter: @BertDecker
Bert is a well-respected communications coach and author. His blog regularly features communications commentary on political and current events.

Olivia Mitchell: Speaking About Presenting
Twitter: @OliviaMitchell
Consistently high quality; this is one of my favorite blogs.

Nancy Duarte: Slide:ology
Twitter: @nancyduarte
Companion to the bestselling Slide:ology book (listed above). Nancy Duarte and other members of the Duarte Design team contribute regularly.

Ian Griffin: Professionally Speaking
Twitter: @cheshirelad
Ian's blog regularly features interviews with professional speakers as well as insights from his experiences with the National Speaking Association.

---

12 Recommended blogs come courtesy of Andrew Dlugan of Six Minutes www.sixminutes.dlugan.com/public-speaking-blogs/.

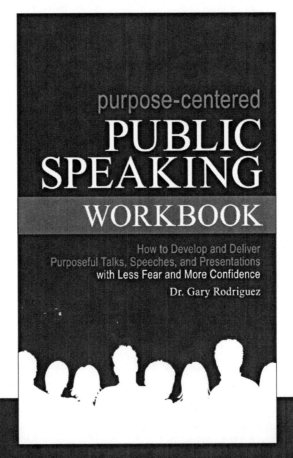

This workbook is a companion to the book
PURPOSE-CENTERED PUBLIC SPEAKING.
It is a practical tool designed to assist you in
preparing purposeful talks.

For information on pricing and bulk discounts
for training large groups - visit us online.
www.LEADERMETRIX.com

Breinigsville, PA USA
14 February 2011
255421BV00001B/1/P